THE KANAZAWA YEARS

*Reminiscences by Michael Randall,
7th Dan, on a golden age
in British karate*

GW00992319

OTHER BOOKS BY CLIVE LAYTON

Conversations with Karate Masters
Unmasking the Martial Artist
Mysteries of the Martial Arts
Mind Training for the Martial Arts
Training with Funakoshi
Karate Master: The Life & Times of Mitsusuke Harada
Shotokan Dawn: Vol. I (in press)
Shotokan Dawn: Vol. II (in press)
A Shotokan Karate Book of Facts: Vol. I
A Shotokan Karate Book of Facts: Vol. II
A Shotokan Karate Book of Facts: Vol. III (in press)
Reminiscences by Master Mitsusuke Harada (in press)

THE KANAZAWA YEARS

*Reminiscences by Michael Randall, 7th Dan,
on a golden age in British karate*

BY

DR. CLIVE LAYTON

SHOTO PUBLISHING

26 POYNTER ROAD, ENFIELD, MIDDLESEX, EN1 1DL, ENGLAND

First Published in 1998
by **Shoto Publishing**, 26 Poynter Road, Enfield,
Middlesex, EN1 1DL, ENGLAND
Tel: 0181-366-2282

**British Library Cataloguing-in-
Publication Data.**
**A catalogue record for this book is
available from the British Library.**

Hardback Edition   ISBN 0 9530287 2 0
Paperback Edition ISBN 0 9530287 3 9

Dedication

TO

RACHEL, PANDORA AND CEDAR

Acknowledgements

The author and publisher would like to thank the following people for their assistance in the preparation of this book: Rachel Layton; Robert Randall, Miyoko Randall and Marty Randall; Hirokazu Kanazawa, 9th Dan, Chief Instructor to Shotokan Karate International; Vernon Bell, 9th Dan, Chief Instructor to Tenshin-Shinyo-Ryu Jujitsu (European Jujitsu Union), 3rd Dan Karate-Do, 3rd Dan Judo; Nicholas Adamou, 7th Dan, Chief Instructor to the International Association of Shotokan Karate; Frank Riley, 4th Dan; Terry Wingrove, 7th Dan, Federation of All Japan Karate Organizations; Prof. Patricia Lister, 3rd Dan; Susan Chalk, 3rd Dan; Mark Hooper, 3rd Dan; Anthony Kirby, 1st Dan.

Photo credits: Roger Hall, 164, 165; Clive Layton, 26, 27, 48, 55, 104, 106, 117; Rachel Layton, 195; William Mannion, 81, 83, 84, 128, 129, 130, 131; Michael Nursey, 126 (top), 127, 139, 166 (bottom), 193; Shoto Publishing photographic library, 21, 32, 33, 40, 42, 43, 44, 45, 54, 58, 60, 61, 62, 63, 67, 75, 86, 89, 91, 93, 94, 96, 100, 101, 107, 110, 111, 112, 114, 115, 116, 118, 119, 121, 123, 124, 126 (bottom), 133, 134, 135, 137, 138, 141, 142, 144, 146, 147, 149, 150, 152, 153, 155, 158, 159, 160, 162, 163, 166 (top), 167, 175, 178, 179, 182, 186, 190, 191; Unknown, 50; Yorkshire Post, 188.

Front cover calligraphy – Miyoko Randall

Contents

Foreword

I was pleased to hear that Dr. Layton has now written a book about the early years of training in Shotokan Karate-do in England, as told by Michael Randall, who was to become one of my finest students. I have read the final draft and I am very impressed with its contents, the stories and anecdotes, and the good-humoured way in which it is written is truly indicative of those days. I am extremely honoured that the book is entitled, *The Kanazawa Years*. I am very surprised that Mr. Randall, with mature spirit, technique, mind and body, did not actually produce such a book sooner.

When I think back to April, 1965, when I went to England to instruct in karate for the first time, I recall Mr. Whitcher, Mr. Randall, Mr. Adamou, Mr. Peachey, Mr. Mannion, Mr. Carpenter, and many more who were my original students. Also, Mr. Sherry, Mr. O'Neill, Mr. Poynton, etc., who enthusiastically came to the London *dojo* from Liverpool, regularly. They were all just boys at the time. I feel very nostalgic, but in the same breath I am so proud that they have become world famous instructors of Karate-do. Especially, Mr. Randall, who is truly a good friend, and one with whom I lived under the same roof on numerous occasions. He is indeed an exceptional person, whose mind lives every day with the spirit of Karate-do.

Traditional Japanese culture, such as that found in Karate-do, has become widespread throughout the world today. For this reason, I believe that this book will make an important contribution, not only to karate students of the United Kingdom, but to karate-ka world-wide, who have devoted themselves to this fascinating art.

30th November, 1997   Hirokazu Kanazawa,
                             9th Dan, Chief Instructor to SKI

Preface

Michael Randall was born in Stoke Newington, North London, on the 8th April, 1944, the eldest of two children to Robert Randall and his wife Vera (née Briton). As an infant, Michael was lucky to surive his first year, for a German V1, colloquially known as a doodle-bug, exploded near the family house during one of the frequent air raids. At the moment this happened, Michael's mother was frantically seeking shelter in the basement, carrying her young son in her arms. The V1's impact caused a violent gas explosion, and as she passed the gas meter by the basement stairs, it was ripped away from its mounting and flew with deadly speed across the narrow landing, missing Michael's head by inches. But then, the gods had other plans for this young man.

Life, after the war, was much the same for the Randall's as for any other working class London family – poor, but relatively happy. As a child, the young Michael clambered and played with his neighbourhood friends over the grey, derelict sites and bombed gutted buildings, whilst his parents eked out a modest living. Robert Randall had been a gunner during the war, serving in Greece, and after demobolization took up employment as a chair frame maker, carrying on the family tradition of working in wood. He took great pride in his craft and acquired a deep affinity with the material his hands turned and shaped. Vera Randall became a highly skilled machinist, a "sample-hand", responsible for dresses to a reputable fashion house.

At school, quiet, shy and retiring, Michael was blighted by two serious setbacks – ill health and a lack of stable schooling. He suffered from asthma from an early age and had two extremely distressful and prolonged bouts of rheumatic fever, for which he was hospitalised. The family moved from rented accommodation to rented accommodation in London and Essex, the children (Michael and his sister, Patricia) having to change schools rather too regularly. This lack of educational continuity, not to say stability and security, quite naturally took its toll, to the extent that when he left Warren Secondary Modern School, Dagenham, aged fifteen, he had not a single examination to his name. This was an unfortunate state of affairs, and one arrived at through circumstances rather than any obvious lack of ability. He had a great interest in anything technical or mechanical, and was an avid reader. He would come top of his form in science and, upon reaching the minimum compulsory leavers' age, intended to enter the field of electronics, but this was quite impossible, for his mathematical ability was simply not up to the required level.

In 1959 then, school behind him, he started work on his fifteenth birthday. Trying his hand at a number of assorted jobs for short periods, including working in an electrical components factory, as a tailor's cutter, and as an apprentice electrician, Michael attempted to find his niche in life. Eventually, some two years later, his father guided him into a seven year apprenticeship as a carpenter and joiner at Union Cold Storage, who were based at Blackfriars and Smithfield, in London. It was there, in 1963, amongst the high jinks and sport of evading work, that he met a seasoned ex-paratrooper, Ray Fuller, who was employed as a painter in the firm's maintenance department. It was a suggestion from Raymond Edward Fuller that completely changed Michael's life, giving it direction and great purpose.

From such humble and unremarkable beginnings then, emerged one of the highest ranking and most respected Shotokan karateka in Britain. Today, Michael Randall holds the esteemed grade of 7th Dan, having been a dedicated black-belt for more than thirty years. His lineage, the basis of this book, is an enviable one, and second to none. He knew Vernon Bell, the man responsible for introducing karate to Great Britain, well, and was a member of the first karate association in this country. He trained regularly at the Horseshoe pub *dojo* – regarded as without doubt the most important and influential training hall in Britain at the time – and was fortunate enough to practise under the great Tetsuji Murakami. It is also believed that Michael is one of only three men, still training in Shotokan in Britain, who can claim to have been taught, in 1964, by Master Hiroo Mochizuki – the first karate instructor to have visited Europe (in 1956). Michael featured in the first karate colour film ever taken in Britain, also in 1964, which was shown in cinemas the length and breadth of the land. These, then, were in the days before the official arrival of the Japan Karate Association.

Michael Randall took part in the vitally important lesson to impress upon the visiting Kazuo Nagai, the eagerness and sincerity of British Shotokan students, and the need for a resident Japan Karate Association instructor to this country. He was also part of the team that gave the first demonstrations ever given in Great Britain by the JKA, supporting Masters Kase, Kanazawa, Enoeda and Shirai, to promote Shotokan. Michael became a select student of Hirokazu Kanazawa – one of the master's Seven Samurai – and was a founder member of the Karate Union of Great Britain. Becoming one of the first in this country to be awarded a JKA black-belt, he committed himself to training, virtually every day under Kanazawa, for three years, before the master left for Dusseldorf and Cologne on his way back to Japan.

This book then, essentially covers personal recollections from the years 1964 to 1968, which is, unquestionably, a golden period in the history of British Shotokan karate. A chapter on the year or so before Master Kanazawa's arrival, in 1965, has thus been included. This not only sets the scene for the main body of this work, but shows that it was because Michael had the solid foundation of the British Karate Federation behind him, that he was able to excel under the Japanese. The chapter's inclusion also provides an interesting history lesson in its own right, and new stories and facts have emerged.

As that which precedes is important, so too is what follows. Thirty years have elapsed since Kanazawa ceased residing in Great Britain, and it was felt that in order to round the book off nicely, readers might like to know the outcome of Michael's training with the master, all these years on. A two part, 'Kanazawa Legacy – A Very Personal View', therefore concludes the work.

Because of the nature of the remit of this book – reminiscences – much has been made of lengthy direct quotes from Michael Randall. Indeed, bar a few 'interruptions' by the author, and small, but significant contributions from Vernon Bell and fellow Shotokan 7th Dan, Nicholas Adamou, the work reads like a monologue. It was felt that to adopt such an approach, to allow Michael the maximum freedom of expression, would not only give greater reliability and validity to the book, but also generate a certain freshness to readers as, in particular, Michael's exceptional personality and character shine through.

Few karateka have devoted themselves to the Way of the "empty-hand" to the extent and depth of Michael Randall. None have been so selfless in the pursuit of their art. His like appears very infrequently. Among the many hundreds of thousands of Shotokan students in Great Britain that have trained over more than forty years, only three, at the time of writing, are believed to have achieved his rank. Of course, as the years tick by, more 7th Dans will surely emerge, but none, I believe, will be able to claim such a deep and distinguished an early training, and offer such a unique perspective – to genuinely be an integral part when British karate history was being shaped.

When Michael started training, there was one BKF Shotokan *dojo* in London and one in the home counties. If you didn't like the hard training there, under the country's most senior grades, then the nearest BKF *dojo* was two hundred miles away in Liverpool, where the training was, no doubt, equally demanding. Only the strongest and most determined survived, and it gave some, a very select few who came through, and genuinely continued, a view of training and a philosophy of life that appears to be sadly almost lost. This book provides a glimpse into another time – a time that many real karate-ka reflect back to, and wish could be again.

September, 1997   Clive Layton, 6th Dan

Preamble

A brief synopsis of the history of British Shotokan, to January, 1964, and the commencement of this work, was deemed to be in order, so that readers, unfamiliar with the topic, might gain a proper perspective, and thus place the contents of this book into its correct historical context. A full history of shotokan karate to this date, is given in the author's two volume, *Shotokan Dawn*.

Vernon Bell, a professional 3rd Dan judo instructor, had trained in Yoseikan karate, in Paris, under Henri Plee and Master Hiroo Mochizuki. On the 13th March, 1957, Bell was awarded his black-belt, becoming the first British karateka to be so honoured. The following month, Bell established the British Karate Federation, which was aligned to the French karate authorities. Throughout 1957, he taught a small, select group of students in the garden of his parents' chalet bungalow at 12, Maybush Road, Hornchurch, Essex; performed the first karate demonstrations in this country; appeared in local newspapers, and, amazingly, even on national television, with visiting guest instructor, Hoang Nam. It was also in December, 1957, that the first 3rd kyu grades were awarded, though in those early days, a six kyu system operated. Then, at the beginning of 1958, Bell acquired the first karate *dojo* in Britain, in St. Mary's Road, Upminster. Training in London began in the middle of that year above the Wheatsheaf pub in Kenton Road, not far from Russell Square. It was also in 1958 that Bell trained privately with Master Tetsuji Murakami, in Paris. Murakami, the first Japanese karate master to visit these shores, arrived in the summer of 1959, at Bell's invitation, and Bell was graded to 2nd Dan. In 1960, Michael Manning was awarded 1st kyu, but would grade no further.

Until about 1960, there were only two British Karate Federation clubs in Britain. The first karate summer school was held in 1959 in Scarborough, as was the 1960 summer school. The 1961 summer school changed venues to St. Osyth's, Essex, and was influential, though, as in the previous two annual courses, only a handful of students attended. A Liverpool BKF *dojo* opened up about this time under Fred Gille, followed by York (under Gordon Thompson) and

Middlesbrough (under Fred Kidd and Walter Seaton). The first BKF *dojo* in Scotland (at Saltcoats) opened as a result of the St. Osyth's course, as did one based at RAF Scampton, in Lincolnshire. *Dojo* appeared in Blackpool and Leicester in 1962, and Bradford and Aberdeen in 1963. Bell also taught members of the Parachute Regiment and USAF personnel at this time. By January, 1964, however, the Leicester *dojo*, all the Armed Forces *dojo*, and the Saltcoats *dojo* had ceased to be BKF affiliated, and are believed to have all closed down.

In London, at the beginning of 1964, training was based above the Horseshoe Pub, in Clerkenwell. Following on from the famous martial arts display, given by the British Budo Council at the Royal Albert Hall, on the 23rd November, 1963, Shotokai master, Mitsusuke Harada, had recently arrived from Belgium, and had just given a course at the BKF London headquarters, at Bell's invitation. The highest BKF grade, in Britain, with the exception of Bell, was 1st kyu, and there were two of these, both training at the Horseshoe *dojo*. Therefore, there was, it is believed, only one British Shotokan black-belt living in England at the time, and less Shotokan branches operating throughout the entire land, than one might find karate clubs today operating in a single sports centre. By January, 1964, there had only been some four hundred and thirty BKF gradings, successful or otherwise, throughout Great Britain. Some students had graded up to six times, so the number of people who had actually graded was incredibly small. It was in this climate that Michael Randall began his study of karate.

I

BEFORE THE COMING OF THE JAPAN KARATE ASSOCIATION

Michael Randall began his story so: "A workmate of mine, Ray Fuller, brought Nishiyama and Brown's book, *Karate the Art of 'Empty-Hand' Fighting*, to work one day and, over our lunch-time sandwiches and cups of tea, he handed me the hardback volume and asked me what I thought. I'd never seen karate before, and indeed I'd never even heard of it, and as I looked through the pages, I thought that it had real potential. I found karate mysterious and absorbing. Ray said that he had heard about it in the army and wanted to try to find a club. He was very enthusiastic and his enthusiasm rubbed off on me. He wanted to know if I was interested in going along with him, and I said that I would be. I didn't go out in the evenings very much. I liked reading at home and listening to music, though I did swim.

"Ray was ten years older than me [born 27th January, 1934]. He had been a signalman in the paras for two years, seen the world, and got into all sorts of mischief. He was an interesting character, full of anecdotes, and I learned a lot from him. He was like a big brother to me, protective. He was a kind-hearted chap, but there was an underlying hardness, and he was not the sort of man you'd pick a fight with in a pub. He was quite physical, and liked to swim and run long distances in his spare time, though he also read and played chess.

"We didn't know who to contact about starting karate, because Nishiyama was in America of course. So, we telephoned the Japanese Embassy and they gave us Vernon Bell's address. We also tried the British Judo Society and the British Judo Association, and they too gave us Bell's address. So, he was obviously our man. This was just before Christmas, 1963. Anyway, Ray drove down one evening to Perryman's Farm Road, Newbury Park, Ilford, Essex, where Bell lived, with me on the back of his motorcycle. I remember it being bitterly cold, even though we had our overcoats on. I should have sat in the sidecar. Sidecars were very popular in those days. We knocked on the door of number 91, and the door opened, but nobody appeared. A woman was standing behind it, in the pitch dark, but she didn't show her face.

"Is it possible to speak to Mr. Bell?" we asked.

The woman was obviously very frightened, and we later learned that she wasn't mentally very well, but she said we had to write to Bell, and abruptly shut the door.

"Well, we did write, and a week or so later we got a letter back. Essentially, it said that we had to write again for details and enclose ten shillings [50p] each, which was a lot of money in those days. We sent the money off with a short covering letter and, about a week later, a large brown envelope packed full of information fell through the letterbox at the family flat in Stoke Newington.

"We couldn't just start karate in those days – nothing like that. We had to become members of the British Karate Federation first, and in order to be considered, Ray and I had to apply for membership by filling in an application form each, sign a Declaration and Oath of Allegiance, get two referees, of which one had to be from a professional person, get a medical certificate to say that we were fit enough to train, and write a letter of application. Everything seemed to be a put off, and I liked that."

Michael Randall's BKF application and Declaration and Oath of Allegiance forms are both dated the 17th January, 1964. Ray Fuller's BKF application form is dated the 20th January, and the Declaration and Oath of Allegiance is dated the following day.

Michael continued: "The things we had to promise in that Oath of Allegiance! I saw one of the old forms not long ago – all about being chivalrous, honoring womanhood, and so on, and to closely guard and protect what we were going to be taught. But it was all deadly serious then, and if you didn't fill the form in, then that was the end of your karate, because Bell wouldn't have let you train. Nearly every one of the fifteen clauses had "as long as I live" at the end of them. What a carry on! However, it was all well intentioned." Certainly, the form was, how shall the author put this, overly comprehensive!

Michael Randall's typewritten letter of application, addressed to Vernon Bell, and dated the 21st January, 1964, has survived, and reads thus:

"I would like to join the BKF, as it is the only official club [association] with qualified instructors in England.

"A friend of mine, Mr. R.E. Fuller, aroused my interest in karate.

Michael Randall at the time of his application to the BKF

After which we bought a book, *Karate By Pictures,* by H.D. Plee. In this book, it clearly states that a qualified instructor is essential for a complete study of Karate-do.

"I am not quite sure how I can contribute to the Karate-do movement, but if I reach a high enough standard, perhaps later on I could be of some use by teaching karate, or in any other way that might be useful."

Michael continued: "Both Ray and I went to the doctors on the same day [15th January, 1964]. I remember Ray's doctor's surname was Richard. My doctor was Dr. Norman Kass. He was based at the Woodberry Down Health Centre, Green Lanes, N4. I liked Dr. Kass. He was a real character too. A large Jewish man. He would make a grand entrance into the surgery in Stamford Hill, smoking a big cigar, blowing smoke everywhere. On one of the walls in the waiting-room there was a large No Smoking sign. He'd just walk past it, puffing away. He used to call me "The Professor", and that was a nickname I had.

"My professional referee, and I think Ray's as well, was the solicitor for the company we worked for. This chap's name was Roberts, and his drab office, papers everywhere, was at 24 to 29 West Smithfield,

B R I T I S H   K A R A T E'   F E D E R A T I O N.
(affiliated to E.K.F.,J.K.A., Yoseikan)

National Coach &
Chairman.
V. C. F. BELL
3 Dan Judo
2 Dan Ju-Jitsu
2 Dan Karate-Do
1 Dan Aiki-Do.

Application for Membership
as
Full/Country/Associate/Member.

No..........

Chief Technical
Adviser.
TETSUGI MURAKAMI
3 Dan Karate-Do
3 Dan Aiki-Do
2 Dan Kendo.

I, (Surname).RANDALL..............(Christian Names)ROBERT, ERIC,MICHAEL
hereby wish to make application for membership of the above organisation and sub-
mit my personal particulars hereunder, for the perusal of the aforesaid Federation.
I confirm that all these particulars are correct and true in every respect, and I
agree, if accepted as a member of this Branch to obey and abide by its Rules and
Regulations, to uphold its Constitution, to conduct myself in a correct manner at
all times (both in and out of the Branch's premises) and to further uphold the
ideals and principals of the science of Karate as laid down by the B.K.F. and by
the Yoseikan by my personal example and co-operation at all times.

Signed.N.Randal.....................
Witnessed.V.G. Randall..........

1. Surname.RANDALL.............Christian Names ROBERT ERIC MICHAEL
2. Permanent address.3, SOUTHWELL HOUSE DOLEYN RD. N.16.LONDON
   16 SLADE RD. Southern Rd
3. Telephone No. (if any)...........3a. Married/Single.SINGLE.....
4. Age..19................4a. Date of Birth..8.4.44....Stoke Newington, N.
5. If under 18 years of age, have you your parents permission to join..........
6. Hobbies/Interests.MUSIC + READING.........................
7. Occupation.CARPENTER + JOINER.......................
8. Service in H.M. Forces - a. period........... b. Service.............
   Rank.................Date of demobilisation............
9. Condition of Health...FIT.............9a. Examiner Pr. M. KH.SS....
10.Date of last medical..15.1.44...........10a. Place of Exam.SURGERY...
11.Have you any Heart/Lung trouble...NO.....Details............
12.Have you High/Low blood pressure......NORMAL...................
13.Do you suffer from any organic, mental or physical disabilities or weaknesses.
   ...NO..........
14.State names and addresses of present Clubs or Societies which you belong to...
   ....
15.Outdoor/Indoor sports played..SWIMMING..................
16.Names/addresses of previous Karate Clubs....................
17.Have you had previous Karate instruction..............a. by whom..........
   ....Place.......
18.Karate Belts held............a. grade.......b. date of grading.....
   ....c. Examiner........d. Any further
   details of Karate experience.............
19.Where did you hear of this organisation..BY..BRITISH..JUDO.....SOCIETY)
20.How and by whom were you introduced.RECOMMENDATION.ON.TELEPHONE
21.State type of instruction desired - Private lessons.NO...Class Instruction.YES
   Complete study of Karate.YES......(Answer Yes or No to above) DEFENSE
22.State precisely why you wish to learn Karate EXCELLENT.FORM.OF.SELF.
23.State how you became interested in Karate and what decided you that a Course of
   training would benefit you INTEREST.FROM A FRIEND........................
   In what way..MENTALY.AND.PHYSICALLY...............

Continued....

Michael's application form to join the BKF

- 2 -

24. Having reached a standard in Karate, to what purpose do you intend using your knowledge. BY CONFORMING WITH B.K.F. REGULATIONS

25. How do you think you can further the science of Karate and in what way...... POSSIBLY LATER ON BY TEACHING

26. Is your interest in this Branch and Karate as a whole -

(a) Theoretical (b) Practical (c) Philosophical (d) Cultural
(e) Scientific (f) Curiosity (g) Knowledge (h) Sport
KNOWLEDGE

27. For how long do you intend participating in Karate AS LONG AS POSSIBLE

28. Approx. days and time available for tuition EVENINGS EXCEPT WED. SAT.

29. Do you intend/desire to take Gradings in Karate.. YES

30. How far in your studies do you intend to go AS FAR AS POSSIBLE

31. Do you intend helping the Branch outside instruction hours.. YES
If so how NOT YET KNOWN   CULTURE;

32. State briefly what your conception of Karate is MENTAL AND PHYSICAL

33. Name/Address of your Sponsor in joining this Branch - MR. V.G. RANDALL
3 SOUTHWELL HOUSE, DOLEYN d N.16

34. Name/address of Seconder in joining MR. D. DAVIS
X a. H. Nightingale 13 Whitehall Lodge N.10 2, Oakington Rd. X
                                                      London W.9

35. I Mr. RANDALL agree to abide by my answers to the above details, and if for any reason I desire to resign my Membership I will do so in writing, stating my reasons, and giving at least one month's notice to the Branch Authorities.

36. I Mr. RANDALL pledge myself at all times to keep and honour my written Agreements with the B.K.F. and by my integrity to keep all verbal and promised arrangements with this Branch forsoever as long as I am a Member.

37. I am fully aware and acquainted with the Constitution, Principles and Objects of the B.K.F. and with the full knowledge of them I desire to become a member. I declare that at all times during my Membership I will to the best of my ability fulfill my obligations as outlined in the Constitution.

Signature. R. Randall.   Date. 17. 1. 64
Sponsor/Witness. V.G. Randall   2nd Witness   X

RECEIVED WITH THANKS.   V. C. F. BELL (2nd DAN)
     2......s.......d.   Chairman/Organiser
per pro BRITISH KARATE FEDERATION.   of British Karate Federation.
     (Karate Club of Great Britain).

M/A/R sent.... 4/1/64   Application.. 17/1/64
G/C sent... 18/1/64 ..No. 396   Refused........Accepted 4/1/64
LIC. issued no. 488 ..4/1/64   Interviewed.. 9/.. Time 28/1/64
E.K.F. Lic. Fee paid   Enrolled... 4/1/64
Full/Country/Ass. Member granted. 4/1/64   A.F. Completed. 17/1/64
                   No. 654   Fee paid.. 28/1/64 .Amount. 2-2-0
 "   "   "   " transferred   Resigned.........Cause
            Period   Dismissed........Cause

per 3 M(c/F/1/A for 11/1/64 - 28/4/64 (2 yrs Creature)
                              - 3/5/64
LRF sent 15/12/64 ARF Pol 16/2/65.
                        ARF '66 sent 14/12/65

23

London, EC1."

Mister Roberts' reference has also survived, dated the 20th January, 1964, and reads thus:

"I have been asked to give a reference in regard to Robert Eric Michael Randall of 3, Southwell House, Boleyn Road, London, N.16, as to his suitability to join the above association.

"I have known Mr. Randall for about three years, during which time he has been in one job and I have always found him sober, honest and trustworthy."

Michael Randall continued: "My other BKF reference came from a plumber I knew. He was a nice tubby guy, a friend of the family. He was well-spoken and had high principles." This reference has also survived. It is from a Mr. W. Stubbington of W. Stubbington and Company, of 67, Mount Pleasant Lane, Clapton, London, E5. Dated the 21st January, 1964, the brief reference reads:

"This is to certify that I have at all times found Michael Randall to be honest and trustworthy."

Michael continued: "During the period this form filling was going on, Ray and I would practise what we could out of the books we'd brought for lunch times. We also had E.J. Harrison's, *The Manual of Karate*. Lunch times were the only occasions we had to practise really. Ray was married and living in Walworth – 67, Lion Street, SE 17, if memory serves me correctly.

"Anyway, the time came to visit the London *dojo*, to actually see a karate class and to meet Mr. Bell. I remember that night very well. Ray and I were both very excited. After work, we went on Ray's bike to the Horseshoe pub at 24, Clerkenwell Close, London, EC1. It was perishing cold on that bike that January evening too, and we didn't have any crash helmets. We just used to wrap scarves around our necks and brave it out. The surrounding area around the Horseshoe has changed a great deal over the last thirty-four years. In those days a lot of Italians lived in the area. Clerkenwell Close was like something out of Dickens. The buildings around the Horeshoe were all Olde Worlde, friendly, with wooden upper floors. It was like a scene from a Christmas card. It was as though we'd been beamed to another time. That really struck me because it was in such contrast to the busy main roads we'd come along. Clerkenwell Close was impressive, different, and what we were about to do was different too. There were no yellow lines in those days or anything like that, and Ray parked his bike right outside the pub.

"We entered the smoke-filled bar and asked the bartender where the karate was being held. He pointed upstairs and then to the door leading to the stairway. Those stairs haven't changed at all – still cold stone. We could hear the sounds in the *dojo* above and it was at this time, at the bottom of those stairs, that my excitement turned to nervousness. We nudged each other forward. Then we heard a *kiai*, and that gave us a bit of a shock. We thought, "What the hell's going on!" You just didn't hear people yelling like that, in unison, in a public house, or anywhere else for that matter, in those days. Anyway, we pushed open the swing doors into the *dojo* and Vernon Bell came over to us.

"Who are you laddies?" he said, in his usual abrupt, inimitable way, and we explained. "Okay. You can sit and watch."

"So, we sat down on a couple of chairs to the right as you enter the *dojo*, and watched the lesson. All the other chairs had clothes on them and shoes were placed underneath the seats. There were no changing rooms or showers – no luxuries. There were no women trainees then. Ray and I both sat straight in our chairs, alert. We didn't speak. We wouldn't have dared talk. There were about twelve to fifteen students I suppose, and Jimmy Neal was instructing. The lesson went on for an hour or an hour and a half. There were different groups of students practising different things – *kumite* mostly, as I recall. When they did basics, they moved towards the elevated area to our right – back and forth.

"I was most impressed by what I saw, inspired really, a wonderful thing. I'd never been terribly sporty, though I had liked playing cricket at school. I had been a wicket-keeper. You need fast reactions to be a keeper, and I brought that, and good timing, to my training. I liked roller-skating too, and that had given me excellent balance. There was no family history of any marked achievement in sport or anything like that, though my mother and father had been keen cyclists in their younger days, and my mother had liked gymnastics.

"Anyway, as soon as I saw karate, I wanted to do it. I thought to myself, "Here is something I can do for myself, not be hassled by other people, where I can be in control of my own future." Jimmy Neal looked the real McCoy. Bell was sitting over in the corner, by a window, occasionally looking up, with papers spread all over a table. When the students were in lines, they moved towards him.

"There's something else too, though it's hard to explain – to put into words. I found a common chord, no pun intended, between my love of music and the karate I saw. My mother had been very musical and her predisposition to sensitivity has been handed down to me, which I've passed onto my son. [Michael Randall's son, Marty, was hailed as a child prodigy classical pianist, when, at the tender age of four, he

The Horseshoe pub, Clerkenwell

became the youngest soloist ever to perform at the Royal Festival Hall, London. He has appeared on television, worldwide, on numerous occasions, and was awarded a music scholarship to a well-known public school. He currently holds the grade of 3rd kyu in karate]. I suppose it was the art in karate that I initially responded to. Also, later, being

Inside the Horshoe pub *dojo*, as it is today

rather a technical person – for example, as a child I was always taking clocks and other such precision instruments apart and putting them back together again – I would look at the moves of *kata*, and so on, to the nth degree. I had a tremendous facility for attention to detail.

"At the end of the lesson, Mr. Bell walked over to us and said, "Well, what do you reckon?"

"I replied that I liked it and that I really wanted to do it. Then he said something that completely stunned me.

"What makes you think you'll be able to, laddie?"

"I didn't know what to say. I just looked at Ray, and he didn't know what to say either. Then Mr. Bell, seeing that we were flustered, continued:

"You come back again next week, and we'll see."

"As far as I can remember, we had to watch twice before we were allowed to train. That really impressed me. I don't care what anybody says, Bell didn't do it for the money. He did everything to put us off – really. I've always considered him to be a purist. He was trying to establish karate in Great Britain and he was doing his best to give it good foundations. That's what all the form filling was about, and all the inconvienice with acquiring references. I take my hat off to him for that."

Bell's little chats with Michael and Ray were their official interviews. British Karate Federation documentation notes the date to have been the 28th January, 1964, at 9.00 pm, when the annual Full Member BKF fee of two guineas (two pounds and two shillings {£2.10p}) was paid over by each. Both students were officially accepted on the 4th February, 1964.

Vernon Bell confirmed Michael's story and wrote of his first impressions of his young student, so: "Mick Randall first came to my London *dojo* of the British Karate Federation, at the Horseshoe pub, in Clerkenwell, in January, 1964. He joined the BKF under licence along with Ray Fuller ... In particular, Michael Randall impressed me greatly by his quiet charm, clean appearance, dignity, courtesy, serious respect, appreciation, and total willingness to learn this very serious art ... He struck me as being a man of honour with total sincerity of purpose. I thought that he would be a distinct benefit to the BKF."

Michael continued: "Before we could start training, we had to have two sponsors from within the club. Both Ray and I had the same sponsors - Brian Hammond and Arthur Nightingale. [Hammond and Nightingale had applied to join the BKF in 1960 and 1963, respectively].

"On our first night, Ray and I trained in loose trousers and shirts. You couldn't really buy karate *gi* anywhere. Many people wore judo *gi*, as did Jimmy Neal. Later, my mother made my first karate *gi*. I was just a bag of nerves that first evening – terrified actually. It was the unknown. Ray was in control though. We were shown *choku-zuki*, and we practised that for some time, then *gedan-barai*. We practised both techniques just standing. Then we were shown *zenkutsu-dachi*. We had to place our hands on our hips and practise moving forward and backwards in the stance, continuously. We didn't have to use our hips in those days though, nobody understood the fundamental importance of the hips at that time.

"After the lesson, we went downstairs to have a drink with the other students. Neal came over and asked us what we'd like. I didn't drink, so I just had a lemonade or something, whilst Ray had a brown and mild. Straight away we were made to feel at home. We asked questions about karate, as beginners do, and they were answered. There was a kind of family atmosphere about the club, and that was really very nice. Vernon Bell never stayed for a drink. I liked Jimmy Neal straight away. He was serious, warm, helpful and very encouraging. I found him to be a first-rate teacher.

"There were some famous karateka to be training at that Horseshoe *dojo* then. Apart from Bell, who, I believe, was the only karate black-belt in Britain at the time, Jimmy Neal and Terry Wingrove held the 1st kyu grade, and were the only two to hold such BKF grades. I never knew much about Wingrove, though I know he lived in Southgate. Wingrove's karate was excellent, as was his jujitsu, but I found him to be fidgety and more distant. Jimmy Neal was a roof tiler. They both started their karate training under Bell in 1959, so they had been prac- tising about four and a half years when I began. I suppose both Wingrove and Neal were in their early to mid twenties, with Neal the elder of the two. I remember Jimmy Neal teaching us more often than Wingrove.

"John Chisholm was a rigger over at Elstree Studios. He met the film stars, daily. He'd been training a couple of years and was close to thirty years old when I started. His karate was impressive and he some- times taught us. He had stiff ankles though. He was a nice guy, friendly, jovial.

"Rob Williams and Eddie Whitcher had been training about a year. They were both in their early twenties. Rob was a grocer and lived over in South Harrow. Eddie was in commercial art, lived over in Hitherfield Road, Dagenham, and was to become a very great friend. Both Rob and Eddie had practised a little judo, and Rob Williams was keen on weight-lifting, I think. Eddie was a tall man, about six foot three, maybe six foot four inches, and both men were very strong. I believe Rob Williams and Eddie held the grade of 5th kyu, blue-belt, when I started, or were graded so shortly afterwards. Williams was a formidable char- acter, but a likeable, friendly sort of chap. Eddie was the only man who could handle him, apart from the two 1st kyu of course. Eddie was quiet, a very private person, who never pushed himself forward.

"I also remember a few other members who had graded when I started. Brian Harper also lived over in Dagenham, and worked for the Ship Carbon Company of Great Britain – strange what you remember! I never knew exactly what he did, but I think it was something to do with radiography or machines. He was approaching thirty when I first met him. He'd just taken his 6th kyu grade, the first grading in those days, a few months before, and passed. He was another nice chap.

"Royston Merrick was an electrician who had started about the same time as Eddie Whitcher. Merrick had graded at the end of 1963. He was also a 6th kyu. He'd been in the marines, I believe, and was in his early twenties when I first knew him. I remember Merrick because I paired up with him for freestyle. I didn't have a clue what I was doing and just launched a barrage of attacks at him. It must have been awful, really scrappy.

"I liked old Arthur Nightingale too. He was in his mid forties and a

6th kyu when I started training. He was a decent man, quiet too. He lived in St. Albans and was a librarian. He'd come into the *dojo* very smartly dressed, always well turned out. He'd wear a beautifully taylored Burberry overcoat – the sort Kanazawa *Sensei* was later to buy – and he always wore black leather gloves. He had a very neat, Hitler-like moustache, and when he trained, if it was cold, he'd ask permission to practice in socks, which we found hilarious. Because he was older than us, I suppose he felt that he had to make up for it somehow, and he'd tell us that he was a demon at judo, and that if he ever got one of us in a lock on the floor, he would say that he could be devilish. He'd come out with all these odd little words and phrases. Because of all the judo comments he made, we used to call him 'Tiger' Nightingale. We all really liked him – he was a very genuine man. He must be nearing eighty now, if he's still alive.

"About a month after Ray and I started karate, a sixteen year old schoolboy began training at the Horseshoe. His name was Michael Peachey, and we became very good friends. He attended the Abbs Cross Technical School in Hornchurch, lived over at Romford, and had practised judo. He became a clerk after leaving school, but now I understand he has a very fine job in the City, working for a Japanese firm. I was closer in age to Mick than Ray, and we sort of gravitated towards one another, had a lot in common, and ended up doing nearly everything together. His karate was very similar to mine, and he too was interested in the technical details.

"A couple of weeks later, Pauline Laville joined the club. She'd been training up in Middlesbrough under Fred Kidd and Walter Seaton, but she hadn't graded. I believe that she was good at judo, but a woman practising karate was virtually unheard of in those days. We gave her a hard time of it, but, to her credit, she braved it out and stayed.

"Now, the men used to change in the *dojo*, as I've said, but Pauline had to change somewhere else of course. She was a good looking woman, small, with long blonde hair. She was aged about nineteen and was a typist. She changed in a room off the *dojo*, and Ray, who'd just split up with his wife, fancied her. He would rush over and look through the keyhole trying to catch a glimpse as she changed. He teased her, acted a real Jack-the-lad. Later, of course, they married. Pauline became the first woman to obtain a Shotokan black-belt in Great Britain.

"I remember Jasper Lassey because he was black and very dignified. He was well educated, worked for the Ghanaian Diplomatic Service, and was based at the Ghana High Commission in Belgrave Square. He started a couple of months after Ray and I, and I guess was in his late twenties.

"Another well educated student who trained at the Horseshoe was an American, Peter Lebasci. He was an architect from New York, and was working up in Piccadilly. He was also in his late twenties. He started training about the middle of 1964."

Vernon Bell recalled, when speaking about Michael Randall, Ray Fuller, Pauline Bindra [née Laville], Mick Peachey, John Chisholm, Eddie Whitcher, Rob Williams, Brian Harper and Roy Merrick, "to name but a few", that, "They were a fine group of pupils and I was very proud of them, individually, and as a group, for their enthusiasm, keenness, dedication and ambition to learn the original, classical style of old Japanese Shotokan Karate-do."

Michael Randall continued: "About a month after Ray and I had started training we had the most fortunate piece of luck. Vernon Bell had organized for Master Hiroo Mochizuki, the first karate instructor to teach in Europe, to come to Britain. [Master Hiroo Mochizuki was the son of the famous aikidoka, Master Minoru Mochizuki, of the Yoseikan]. He taught us in London and then went up to Gordon Thompson's *dojo* in York, before travelling back to Paris. It was only a brief stay – three or four days. Members of the London *dojo* trained with him twice, on a Friday evening and all day Saturday, but Ray and I were raw beginners really, and he concentrated mainly upon the senior grades.

"Of course I didn't know anything about karate when Mochizuki came over, but he did impress me greatly. I never once saw Bell train, and we took our example from Wingrove and Jimmy Neal. They were good, very good in fact, but Mochizuki was in a different league. His techniques were fast and crisp, but, and I remember this distinctly, he said it was permissible to bend the back leg and lift the heel off the floor in *zenkutsu-dachi*. Now, we had had it drummed into us that you never ever bent your back leg, and never ever lifted your back heel off the floor. A straight back leg and a back foot planted firmly, grounded you, and gave the body a good lock. We all looked at one another, unhappy about it, but we practised it. What we didn't know was that Master Mochizuki, having come to Europe initially a Yoseikan 2nd Dan, had returned to Japan, and had come back a 4th Dan in Wado-ryu.

"However, what impressed me most about Master Mochizuki was the way he conducted himself. He was obviously well educated, refined – a cultured individual. He acted like the perfect gentleman. He didn't try to dominate or override the wishes of others. He was from a far better class of Japanese than some that later came to Britain.

Master Hiroo Mochizuki

Mochizuki spoke French, and Bell and Wingrove spoke French too. Wingrove was talented with languages, and later learned to read and speak fluent Japanese, as did Mick Peachey.

"It occured to me that if I wanted to be as good as the Japanese in a Japanese martial art, I had to think like them. I was intrigued by the "mind like the moon" imagery from Nishiyama and Brown's book, for

Master Tetsuji Murakami

example. I decided that, apart from karate practice, I would try to find out more about Zen, and so on, by reading about it. I liked reading, as I've mentioned, so there was no problem for me. I read D.T. Suzuki's *Essays in Zen Buddhism*, which I think was in three thick volumes. *Zen and the Art of Japanese Culture* was another book, I recall. I wanted desperately to understand the philosophy that drove the Japanese to excel, and I'm sure I got a lot out of those books. I did my best to digest them.

"I also trained with Master Tetsuji Murakami. He was a small man, and that gold tooth was unmistakable when he smiled. He was technically brilliant of course. Bell had advertised him as a 3rd Dan, and that is indeed what he was, but not from the JKA. We later learned that he was a *shodan* of that organization, but he was still fabulous. He'd trained at the JKA before coming to France. He looked as though he'd probably trained everyday since coming to Europe – that was seven years – so he was probably equivalent to a 3rd or 4th Dan at least. I don't think he knew many *kata* though. The senior grades in the BKF held him in high esteem, and that was good enough for me. He was very supple. I recall that we trained outside in the extensive grounds of the Grange Farm Centre, in Chigwell, so that must have been the summer of 1964. He didn't grade anybody though. He had done so in the past of course, but we were all waiting for the JKA to come over and gradings had been temporarily suspended, I believe. There was a lot of politics going on behind the scenes, and even if we had known all about it, I doubt if we'd have fully appreciated it.

"I found Murakami to be a shady character to be quite honest, a bit of a gangster. There was just something about the man I didn't like. I was a little scared of him as well, if the truth be known, for he had a reputation of slapping students hard around the face, and he wasn't averse to knocking them out either. He spoke French too, because he resided in Paris. For all his severity, he was also good for a laugh. When the seniors taught him how to swear, that was a bit awkward at times, very awkward, because he'd practise, not appreciating what he was saying, in public places, thinking he was being polite, thinking that he was being the perfect English gentleman!

"Another funny little story from that time which I shall never forget is this. Bell lorded over everyone in the *dojo*, he was the black-belt, and every night we trained at the Horseshoe a glass of milk would be placed on his table, in anticipation of his arrival. He would drink the milk as he did his paperwork and preside over the training. Picture this if you will. We were all practising away, and Bell took his first gulp of the night. He stood bolt upright and declared, "Gentleman! I've been poisoned!" It was just like a scene from a *Monty Python* sketch. Somebody had apparently put gin in the milk. I think that must have been Terry Wingrove. He was always up to tricks like that. We were all absolutely terrified of Bell, in awe of him, but Wingrove wasn't. Bell glared around the room, searching for the culprit. I was petrified. I thought, "I hope he doesn't think I've done it!" I often reflect on that little story, and I laugh each time. It was surreal.

"I also remember another incident that happened at the Horseshoe *dojo* in the early days. Ray and I hadn't been training very long, when Mr. Bell walked into the *dojo* with a gentleman who looked as if he'd just come from the City. He wore a very smart, expensive suit, and carried a walking stick and briefcase. I suppose he was aged about thirty. "Who's this?" we thought, "He surely can't do karate?" We weren't sure whether to take him seriously or not. He just didn't look the part. Well, this chap just sat quietly by himself, watched the lesson, and when the training was over he got up and started to get undressed. To everyone's amazement he put Bell's black karate *gi* on and black and red belt [the black and red belt was to signify Yoseikan {karate} Dan status]. And we thought, "Who the hell is this guy?" He loosened up and then proceeded to knock the living daylights out of the top grades in the club at freestyle. The seniors were trying to defend themselves whilst avoiding the pillars in the *dojo* – but no chance. He really let them have it. God knows who he was, but it was reassuring that a mild looking chap like that could overcome much larger men by karate technique alone. He floored Rob Williams with a groin kick. I reckon he must have been one of Bell's early students, before 1961, because no one at the *dojo* knew him. I think Bell got him down to keep the higher grades in their places. You know, "You're good, but you're not that good." After he'd pasted everyone, this chap simply got dressed and went off home. I'd very much like to know who he was.

"The rectangular pillars in the middle of the *dojo* are still there, helping to hold the old building up, but if anyone ever feels like going along to the *dojo*, look out of those lovely old windows with the iron guards at the end of the *dojo* diagonal to the newly housed bar, onto the side of the building opposite. Many things may have changed in more than thirty-four years, but that view is exactly the same. Looking at a brick wall is a bit dreary, I suppose, but you can enter the spirit of the time with that.

"Ray and I also ventured to Bell's Upminster *dojo*, the old British Legion Hall in St. Mary's Road, to train on Sunday mornings, but it was a hell of a journey from where we lived, and we didn't go there often. This *dojo* had a tremendous history. For starters, it was the first *dojo* in Britain where karate was ever practised. Master Murakami taught there every time he was over for the BKF. It had a lovely parquet floor surface. Jimmy Neal taught there the first time Ray and I went. It was so cold on Ray's bike that I was still bone cold at the end of the lesson!

We had to practise *uchi-uke* and *gedan-barai* whilst facing a wall for a solid hour. I really liked that type of training. I thought that it was brilliant. But you wouldn't get away with it now.

"At work, at Smithfield, the company owned a large old building. On the ground floor was the workshop, the first and second floors held stock, and the third floor was empty. Ray and I would go up to the third floor and practise there at lunch times. I also remember that we cut up a piece of thick card the size of a person's head. We cut out two holes to represent eyes, and raised it up to head level. We practised *nihon-nukite* with that piece of card for hours, trying to get our fingertips into the holes. We didn't know what we were doing of course. We never practised the technique in karate lessons, we were never taught it, but we must have seen it in a book somewhere. However, one thing we did learn from that exercise was that if you tense your fingers, then you'll almost certainly miss the target. We would keep our fingers relaxed and became quite adept at piercing the target. When there wasn't any work to do, we'd skive off and practise.

"The firm owned a lot of property, and had premises opposite the old workshop. Ray and I discovered a huge, empty, underground room, that must have been a store room in the past, but now had been completely forgotten about. We made this our personal *dojo*, and hung a bag up made from hessian sacks which we filled with wood shavings that we'd taken from the workshop.

"One of the buildings the company owned overlooked Guy's Hospital. Ray and I would get up onto the roof, via a trap door, and practise, and we could see the nurses on the roof opposite, sun-bathing. We used to practise *Heian Shodan* up there. We'd chalk out the *kata's* line of movement and practise it over and over again. We must have done it hundreds of times on that roof, though it didn't do me a lot of good at my first grading, as you'll see. We also practised freestyle. We never practised freestyle in the lessons either, but we were dead keen, even if we didn't have a clue what we were doing. We were still ungraded. We'd face each other from quite a distance and then move towards one another ever so slowly, like they do in the samurai movies. When we got within range, we'd go at each other like a couple of wildcats. It was insane, stupid, but we didn't know any better.

"One day, Ray was up on the roof, practising, and one of the nurses opposite saw this man frantically throwing his arms and legs about, and thought that Ray was a madman and intended throwing himself off the roof. She'd never seen karate before – very few people had – and she called the police. Anyway, a policeman, unbeknown to Ray, came up through the trap door and touched Ray on the shoulder. In a reflex motion, Ray span around and hit him. Ray got the sack for that – not for hitting the policeman, but for practising karate on the roof! I can't remember whether the incident happened during his lunch hour or during his working time.

"We had all sorts of fun on that roof. We used to throw great chunks of moss that we took off the roof by the giant cooling tanks, onto the traffic wardens seven storeys below us. That was great fun. They thought it had fallen from the roof. Ray and I would throw the moss and then charge to the service lifts and cross over the road via a series of tunnels. We'd come out on the other side and watch the commotion we'd caused at street level and say, "What's up?"

"We used to get up to all sorts of pranks. I used to put a stink-bomb at the base of a chair leg in the mess, and when the grumpy old-timers used to come in, the person who sat on the chair would burst the disgusting, foul-smelling bomb. People were accused of polluting the atmosphere. You should have heard the language, and they'd throw tea over one another. There would often be a punch-up, and the huge wooden table in the middle of the room would be lifted up and overturned. Ray and I would have our tea in the workshop, and we'd roar with laughter. We did that trick three or four times and it always had the same hilarious effect.

"Another thing I used to do was to make an excuse and go to the toilet. I'd put sneezing powder down into the room I'd just left via the fan light. We were little devils. Harmless stuff though, just practical jokes, trying to make a good day of it. Anyway, back to the karate!

"The British Karate Federation was the official karate body in Great Britain for the Japan Karate Association. Vernon Bell had been awarded a *shodan* from the JKA in recognition of his training and work. This was a kind of honorary title, for he never graded for it. Bell was desperate to get a top JKA instructor over to Britain, and in May, 1964, Kazuo Nagai came over from Japan as part of a European tour to look at the feasibility of sending such a man. We all knew this, for it had been explained to us, and Bell wanted everyone in the club to turn out and put on a good show for the visiting dignitary. We all naturally assumed that Nagai practised karate, but now I understand that he did not, which, if true, seems a bit strange.

"Bell hired a special hall in South London, though I can't remember exactly where it was, for the sample lesson, and Terry Wingrove took it. There were about forty students there that evening, and that was a big turn-out. We exercised, practised basics, pre-arranged sparring and *kata*.

"Nagai was a small man, smartly dressed – immaculately turned out. He sat next to Bell at a table and watched extremely attentively as we tried our very best. We may not have had anything like the expertise that he was used to seeing in Tokyo, but we were jolly eager, and we hoped that this eagerness would shine through. Ray and I were not wearing karate *gi* – we couldn't get them – and at the beginning of the lesson Bell asked Nagai if it was okay for us to train. He said that it was alright, but at the end made the comment that everybody, without exception, should be wearing a karate *gi*. That was the last we saw of him. Bell took him up to Liverpool and then off he went to Belgium.

"In those days you didn't have to have a certain number of lessons before you could grade, as is common practice today. You graded when your teachers thought you were ready. I think I'm correct in saying that until 1964, 6th kyu was the lowest grade, but when I went for my first grading, at the London *dojo*, on the 4th July, 1964, I was graded to 8th kyu. My licence shows that novice, red-belt, was signed on the same day, so I don't quite know what happened there.

"The grading was much the same as it is today. We lined up, performed basics and *kumite*, and then finished with *kata*. My *kata* was *Heian Shodan*, which, you may recall, I had practised continuously on the roof at work. I thought I knew that form like the back of my hand. As it turned out, I didn't! I got to the last of the three *age-uke*, performed a *kiai*, and caught Bell's eyes. I completely forgot where I was. Bell, who was conducting the grading, was sitting about seven or eight feet away at a wooden table, glaring at me. He was a hypnotist. His black-belt, the sign of his authority, was coiled up on the table to the right of him. I was absolutely mesmerized in that *age-uke* position, frozen, and just stood there. Bell picked his belt up and threw it at me to wake me up, and told me to sit down. I was so terribly disappointed, but I consoled myself, as I watched the others grade, that karate practice was the important thing, not gradings *per se*. I'd failed. Fair enough ... It was my fault. I'd made a mess of it – but I could take it again next time.

"Much to my surprise, at the end of the grading, Bell called me up and asked me to perform the *kata* again. I thought I'd failed and was no longer worried. When you're not worried about being defeated you can do things, and this time I didn't make any mistakes, and Bell passed me. I wore the white belt. In those days, you wore the white belt for 7th kyu as well. A 6th kyu wore a blue belt, as I've said, 5th and 4th kyu wore purple belts. From 3rd kyu to 1st kyu students wore brown belts.

"Ray also passed, as did Pauline, Mick Peachey, Lassey, Lebasci, and about five or six others. So that was good, we were all progressing together, but we didn't grade again for over a year."

Michael Randall's grading success under Bell and the BKF was recorded in the BKF grading register as number 488.

Michael continued: "Ray and I trained at the Horseshoe pub, on that old lino covered floor, for about six months, I suppose, before Bell had to move the *dojo*. It had been the BKF London *dojo* for some three years, and was extremely influential. We had to leave because the ceiling in the bar would bounce up and down as we practised in unison, and the proprietor was fearful that the whole thing would come down upon his customers. You could actually see the plaster boards moving, and as more people began training, so the movement increased.

"The club moved to the Prince of Wales Baths, Kentish Town, on the corner of Prince of Wales Road and Grafton Road. Although the outside of this late Victorian building hasn't changed at all, the hall inside that we used as a *dojo* is no longer there – it's now a swimming pool! As I recall, we entered the baths, for karate, via the Ladies Baths double doors on Grafton Road. The old iron fence is still there, outside. It was a cold, stark, clinical sort of place. The floor was a yellowy stone and extremely cold, and the walls were just painted brick, with large exposed pipes mounted on them. After closing the *dojo* doors, we used to put green screens in front of them so that anybody who opened them would get the message that the people in the hall didn't wish to be disturbed. The *dojo* was far more spacious compared with the cramped surroundings of the Horseshoe, which was a definite plus. I liked the Kentish Town Baths *dojo*, even though it was cold.

"I remember a couple of incidents from those pre-JKA days at the Kentish Town *dojo*, the first of which is rather unsavoury. A very muscular chap joined the club. He was a bodybuilder I think, and was muscle bound. He couldn't do karate properly, couldn't kick very well at all, because of his muscles. Anyway, one evening after training, we all went to the local pub and were sitting around chatting about karate technique, and this chap said something like: "I might not be able to do all those fancy kicks and things, but watch this. See that chap over there? ..." and pointing to a large, stocky, Irish navvy, standing at the end of the bar, strolled over as if he was going to order a drink. I couldn't believe what happened next. This chap we'd been speaking to went up to this big Irishman who was having a quiet drink, and from about three feet away charged at him with a headbutt. The Irish labourer went down like a sack of potatoes, blood everywhere, a broken nose I suppose, at

A famous group photo of members of the London Kentish Town *dojo*, in 1964. From left to right, standing: unknown, Jasper Lassey, Ray Fuller, Vernon Bell, Jimmy Neal, Michael Randall, Michael Peachey; kneeling: Eddie Whitcher, Royston Merrick, Terry Wingrove, John Chisholm, Robert Williams, Brian Harper.

best. The bodybuilder, who was incredibly strong, then went for a large leather chair, the sort you put in the corner of a room. He raised this enormous chair above his head and brought it down on the man he'd floored. Well, fortunately, as he brought it down, the legs got entangled with some heavy velvet curtains that hung over a door, and he pulled the curtains down. He couldn't complete what he'd set out to do, thank God, for if he had, then he'd certainly have killed the Irishman. The labourer was just lying on the floor, face towards the ceiling; a complete stranger. The bodybuilder dropped the chair and was out of the door before you could take a breath. A large number of Irish navvies, all powerful men, appeared suddenly, almost out of the woodwork, to attend to their fallen drinking companion. I was absolutely terrified; such mindless violence. Luckily, this Irishman's mates didn't know the bodybuilder had been with us, because if they had, we would have been for it. We just sat there for a while, and when we thought the time was right, walked out, gingerly.

"This bodybuilder chap also had an altercation with Bell over a female visitor to the *dojo* from Hawaii. She practised karate and had been a student of Kanazawa's, when he was chief instructor to the island. She was an attractive woman, sexy, fairly tall and slender with long dark hair. Her body was toned, and you could see that she practised something with dedication. I remember that her feet looked very strong. Anyway, this chap wanted to take the girl home and Bell, who we reckoned was on very friendly terms with her, said no, and threw the bodybuilder's car keys over a wall. You've got to hand it to Bell, the man had guts, especially given the bodybuilder's violent, not to say unbalanced reputation." [The young lady in question was, almost certainly, Miss Sue Largosa Reed, and the date of the incident can be pinpointed exactly to the 17th July, 1964].

Michael continued: "I also remember a black-belt came to the club, an American, who was in the United States Airforce. He was one of Bob Trias's students and was very good. He was tall, slender and strong, a kind of All American, and that was an image I liked at the time. Vernon Bell, or perhaps it was Wingrove, let him take the lesson. I recall that we spent quite a bit of the time moving up and down the hall in *zenkutsu-dachi*, with our hands upon our hips. I remember thinking that that was what the low grades, like me, practised, and it made me realise that basics were important, irrespective of grade. The lesson was excellent, and at the end, Ray and I walked over to him and asked if he'd perform a *kata* for us, and he did. It was fantastic, though it wasn't a *kata* we'd ever seen before. The *kata* had a jump in it though, like in *Kanku-sho*. We were so impressed that we asked if he'd do another one, and he performed the same *kata* again. I remember that Bell sold Ray and I a good book by Trias at the Kentish Town Baths *dojo*, though the first karate book I ever bought was by Bruce Tegner, another American.

"Ray and I used to go to a secluded glade in Epping Forest and plant a *makiwara* into the soil. We'd take it in Ray's sidecar, along with a heavy mallet. It wasn't a proper, tapered *makiwara*. It was just a four by two [inch] plank cut to the right length, which we'd made in the workshop. We designed a plaited straw pad for it as well. We punched, kicked and struck that *makiwara* for hours. When we'd finished, we'd pull it up, place it in the sidecar again, and off we'd drive.

"I used to do all sorts of things in those days that I thought would help develop my karate. One of the books I read recommended driving your fingers into a bucket of sand. I did this for hours too. Then I progressed to a bucket of millet. I also drove two large masonry pins into my bedroom wall, tied a length of rope between them, and draped a large coconut doormat over the rope, underside facing outwards. It was flush against the concrete wall, and I'd practise *gyaku-zuki* and *oi-zuki*.

Michael punching the *makiwara* in Epping Forest – 2nd August, 1964.

My knuckles blew up and I thought that that was good, and carried on, despite the pain. But it wasn't good. Of course the wall had no give in it, and what I thought was the beginnings of calloused knuckles was nothing more than a lot of fluid. The body was trying to protect itself,

Practising *shuto* on the *makiwara*.

and there I was just whacking it. Madness, absolute madness, but you see I didn't know what I was doing. That was really bad training, and I just succeeded in permanently damaging my right hand knuckles. Even today, more than thirty years on, if I hit anything hard with my right

Michael blocks *osae-uke* and counters *shihon-nukite*.

Michael counters *gedam-kekomi* to Ray Fuller's *mawashi-geri*.

Michael blocks *tate-shuto* and counters with *mae-geri*.

Michael counters Ray Fuller's *oi-zuki* with *tate-shuto*, and responds with a *chudan kekomi*.

hand, it swells and hurts. Most of the breaks I did later on, I did with my left hand.

"I remember another little thing I used to get up to as well. There was a Saturday market in Hackney that I'd go to with a friend of mine, Mervyn, who lived in the first floor flat directly above me. He later took up karate and became a black-belt under Kanazawa. Anyway, I'd buy the old 78 records, which were an old penny each. I used to take them home, stack them, and see how many I could break with a down-ward-punch.

"Training at the Horseshoe pub and the Kentish Town was hard. There was little let up from the constant repetitions, and often the combinations were lengthy. They say a picture is worth a thousand words, and moving pictures must be worth more. I think that if readers were to watch the short Pathe Pictorial film that was taken near Christmas, 1964 [6th November], at the Baths, then they could see exactly what we were practising before the JKA arrived. Watch the hips, or should I say lack of hips. I believe that was the first colour film ever shot in this country on karate. That's a great bit of film – historic and historical. Watching the Pathe Pictorial film again, I remember doing the sequence of *gedan-barai/jodan ren-zuki/chudan ren-zuki/gedan ren-zuki* – that's six punches each combination. Neal and Wingrove certainly kept us at it, though for some reason John Chisholm was leading that sequence in the film. Perhaps, working at the film studios, he'd got Pathe down?

"We all became pretty fit practising karate. In retrospect, the two bouts of rheumatic fever that I'd suffered held me in good stead. They strengthened my resolve. With the illness, the joints became badly in-flamed and swollen. One sweats copiously with rheumatic fever, and my temperature rose alarmingly. Both episodes of the illness were ex-tended and I was hospitalized. I lived on a prescribed cocktail of milk, glucose, fruit juice and penicillin. My joints were wrapped in cotton wool between the frequent sponging down of my body. I was in bed for five weeks on each occasion, before prolonged convalescence. I was most fortunate not to have suffered complications involving my lungs, and more particularly, my heart. There is no question about it, those bouts of rheumatic fever strengthened my resolve, and that was a defi-nite plus in my study of karate.

"That Pathe evening, when we walked into the *dojo*, all the equip-ment was set up and technicians were milling about. You had to be careful of the cables and the lights. The cameraman used a heavy shoul-der camera, and he filmed from different angles. Terry Wingrove and Jimmy Neal were featured, as were Eddie, Ray, Rob Williams,

Chisholm, Harper, Merrick and Mick Peachey. I found myself in the front line with Lassey to my left and Merrick to my right, and the cameraman focussed in on me for some reason during the *mae-geri/kizami-zuki/gyaku-zuki* basic combination. It's all on the film. They asked Vernon Bell to present brown belts to Wingrove and Neal. It was all set up of course, but we're so fortunate that film has survived. The lesson was extended that night by an hour or so, but the film shown lasted less than three minutes.

"I went to see the film at the Savoy cinema, in Kingsland High Road, Stoke Newington. Pathe films came on between the feature and the B movie. The feature film finished, everyone went to the toilet or to get an ice cream, or a drink, and then they'd sit back down and wait for the B picture. That's when the karate film was shown – at the end of the interlude. I remember feeling immensely proud of seeing myself up on that giant screen, and thinking that the packed-out audience were all watching me, and the other lads of course, practising karate. That film was shown to audiences all over the country. I wonder if it went to any other countries? I was sitting in the stalls, very excited – a lovely feeling. [Details of how to acquire the Pathe Pictorial film are given in Volume I of the author's *Shotokan Dawn*].

"Around this time I got married to my girlfriend, Ruth, and moved to 10, Sigdon Road, Hackney, London, E8, in the September of 1964. Six months later we moved to 17, Sydner Road, Stoke Newington, London, N16. Over the next four years we had two daughters, Donna and Paula. During this period my resolve was tested to the extreme. My wife became mentally unstable as a result of giving birth and was in and out of the hospital. It was a terrible time for all of us – very traumatic, very disturbing. Twenty years old and I reckon I was on the edge of a nervous breakdown. This state of affairs went on for years. My karate was vital to me, absolutely vital. I was not only able to vent the frustration by physically punching and kicking, but it gave me something to hold onto when everything else I cared for seemed to be collapsing around me. I don't know what would have happened if I hadn't had a release. It was an awful time for me, a truly awful time. My wife couldn't look after the babies, so my mother had to step in, and she effectively brought them up.

"I was obsessed with karate, and I'll confess something to you now that I've always been ashamed of. The night my wife had our first daughter, I went training. I went training and then visited the two of them in hospital. I'm not proud of that. But you see, karate was my life, and to miss training was just something I couldn't do.

47

The Prince of Wales Baths, Kentish Town

"Another little story, which happened slightly later, I've told before [in *Shotokan Dawn*]. It involved my wife again and it tells you how I felt about Bell, as well. I was at work one day and I got a phone call to say that Ruth had been taken ill and was hospitalized. It was the usual problem, but it was bad this time because the doctors had admitted her immediately. I decided that I couldn't go training, so I suppose I had learned an important lesson. During my lunch-hour, I ran to the nearest telephone, which seemed to be miles away, and rang Vernon Bell. You were obliged to report to him if you couldn't train. If you didn't inform him of an intending absence, there was hell to pay the next time you trained. It wasn't about money, because you paid in advance. As I say, Bell ran a good *dojo*. I was so worried about ringing him. We were all frightened of him, and I was shaking when I telephoned. I was also dreadfully worried about Ruth, though I knew that she was in the best place. Bell picked the phone up, but because I was in such a state, I could only mumble and splutter. Eventually, I got some kind of message through. He was just silent on the other end of the line, then said a few words and put the phone down. That made me in a worse state, and I fretted the afternoon away thinking about my poor wife and ringing Bell again in my tea-break. Bell agreed to my absence that evening, but I'll never forget that dreadful day. [The telephone number that Michael rang that afternoon was Valentine 7705].

48

"A number of students started at the Kentish Town Baths around this time who were to become well known or subsequently famous. Just after we moved to the new *dojo*, two students started whose names were very similar, and that's one reason why I remember them – Jack Johnson and John Johnston. Jack was a chemist in his mid twenties, who lived in South London. He was a typical Aussie – big, strong, friendly. Jack took his training very seriously, and we became good friends, as you'll see. John Johnston was about the same age as Jack and worked in the City, in advertising, I believe. Without doubt, however, the most famous to be, were the Adamou brothers, Nick and Chris. Nick now teaches worldwide, and I consider him to be one of the finest instructors around today. They were to become very close friends too. When they joined the *dojo* in December, 1964, they were both employed as clerks in London and lived over in Wood Green – Granville Road, I think. Chris was the elder of the two by a couple of years."

At the time of writing, it is believed that there are three British Shotokan 7th Dans – Andrew Sherry, Michael Randall and Nicholas Adamou (7th Dans awarded in that order). Nick Adamou, who was kind enough to share his early memories of Michael Randall with the author, and is sporadically quoted throughout this book, recalled visiting the BKF London *dojo* and his initial, very favorable impressions of Michael Randall, so:

"The very first time I ever saw Karate-do being practised was when I visited the Prince of Wales Baths, Kentish Town, in December, 1964, just before I started karate practice myself. Amongst those present in that class, which was being taught by Terry Wingrove, who was a brown-belt, were Eddie Whitcher, Robert Williams, Royston Merrick and Brian Harper ... There were also two other students in this class, and these were Mick Peachey and Mick Randall, both white-belts ... Although there were brown and purple-belts in that session, I was instantly drawn to the manner in which Mick Randall behaved in the lesson. There was a humbleness and innocence in his whole demeanour, on the one hand, and yet even to my untrained eye at that time, I thought his techniques were brilliant – a fact that was to be verified as I became experienced over the years."

Michael Randall continued: "The last thing I remember at the Kentish Town *dojo* before the JKA came over, was when John Smith of the *Daily Mirror* came down with a photographer on the 30th January, 1965. I've still got the cutting. The single photo shows John Smith standing and Terry Wingrove kicking to his head. Smith just froze, and Wingrove kicked. If you look closely, I'm at the back sparring with

BKF instructor, Terry Wingrove, performs a kick upon reporter, John Smith –
January, 1965. Partly obscured behind Wingrove's kick are John Chisholm
(who is kicking), and Michael Randall. Behind John Smith is Michael Peachey.
In the top left-hand corner, Vernon Bell (very indistinct) talks to a group of
white-belts.

someone unseen, next to John Chisholm.

"Later, of course, we had to leave the Kentish Town Baths too. One
evening the caretaker, I think, marched in during the lesson and asked
us to depart. I can't remember if we were running late, though I suspect
we were. Bell took great exception to this chap's attitude and actions
and chased him out of the hall. Bell wouldn't have it, and that was the
end of that!

"When I started training, there was talk of the JKA coming over, as
I've mentioned. Nagai had apparently given a good report on British
karate, and Bell told us, in early 1965, that four JKA instructors would
be visiting in April as part of a world tour, and one would be staying.
Ray and I attended a film showing of JKA karate in a school classroom
in Ilford, early in 1965, that Bell had set up for BKF members. He had
a few films like that which he'd acquired from Tokyo, and charged us
a few bob [shillings] to watch them. They were silent, black and white,
on 8mm. We'd never seen anything like it. The speed and the power
were phenomenal. We were like bushmen seeing a jumbo jet for the
first time. We were totally awe inspired. It's difficult for people to un-

derstand that type of feeling today, because everybody has seen some form of karate, if only on television, but when we saw that film it was like seeing our very first aeroplane, and we were more than a little shocked.

"Bell was desperate to get the Japanese over, and so were we. Things were hotting up on the political and business front as well. Master Harada of the Shotokai was now resident, and Boulton had come back from Japan a *shodan* in Kyokushinkai from Matsutatsu Oyama. Tatsuo Suzuki of the Wado-ryu had arrived in the country at the beginning of 1965, and Masafumi Shiomitsu would arrive in the summer of that year to act as his assistant. The BKF had already lost students to Wado-ryu, the most notable being Walter Seaton and the Middlesbrough *dojo*. It seemed vital that Shotokan was represented by the Japanese as well, otherwise the other styles would get the lion's share of things. There was a lot of politics going on – people carving out territories for themselves, that sort of thing.

"So, it appeared that we really were going to have a top Japanese Shotokan karate-ka based in London, but what we didn't know at the time was that the face of British Shotokan would change forever as a result."

II

THE MASTERS ARRIVE AT LAST

Michael Randall continued: "Bell needed to get work permits for the visiting Japanese party so we knew the names of the instructors before they arrived. The first we saw of them was on the evening of the day they flew into Heathrow from France. That was at the end of April, 1965. The four instructors were Taiji Kase, Hirokazu Kanazawa, Keinosuke Enoeda and Hiroshi Shirai. Great Britain was the last leg of a tour that took in the USA and Europe.

"Bell had acquired a new *dojo* a few minutes walk from the Kentish Town Baths, in anticipation of an increased number of students as a result of the arrival of the Japanese. That was good thinking, for numbers did rise dramatically. We still trained at the Kentish Town Baths as well at this time, and indeed continued to do so for about another six or seven months. The new *dojo* was at Lyndhurst Hall, in Weldon Road, just off Grafton Road. There were two halls at Lyndhurst Hall, and for that first night Bell had hired the larger *dojo*. After work, I rushed home full of excitement, had some dinner, and got to the *dojo* in good time. It was an excellent turn out as I recall, and we all had high hopes. It was a culmination of years of work on Bell's part and a lot of wishing on ours.

"I can't remember if we were training or not when Bell walked in with the JKA instructors, though I think that we almost certainly were. I believe Jimmy Neal was taking the lesson, but it could have been Terry Wingrove. Bell walked into the *dojo* and we all naturally looked towards the door, which was in front of us and to our extreme left. We were all practising with the stage to our right, looking forwards. The Japanese bowed in, one after the other, carrying their kit bags, looking resplendent in their clean white karate *gi*, contrasting black belts and brown complexions. Remember, I'd only ever seen two Japanese wearing black belts in over a year, and only one

Lyndhurst Hall

Caucasian, and none of them were as good as these men. Here then, suddenly, in our little *dojo*, were four, all at one time! Two of them were former Grand Champions of the JKA and one a former JKA *kumite* champion. They were effectively world champions. [Kanazawa had won the first JKA *kumite* title in 1957 and had been Grand Champion {winning both *kumite* and *kata* titles the same year} in 1958 – the year of the famous four extensions of time during the *kumite* final between Kanazawa and Mikami, which resulted in the only JKA Championship draw. Shirai had been Grand Champion in 1962, and Enoeda won the *kumite* title in 1963. Master Kase, being senior, had been a judge and referee].

"Bell introduced them, one by one, starting with Kase, and they bowed in turn. We were all very impressed before they even did a thing. They were upright and proud, confident in their abilities. They exuded superior ability. They were superior men. I was awe struck to be honest, and I don't think for a moment that I was the only one. I was nervous too. Not frightened of them really, or anything like that, but having people of that calibre in our midst was just a wonderful feeling. You could sense their power before they even did any karate. Kase, who was the oldest [thirty-six] was obviously in command. He was short and stocky, and held the rank of 6th Dan, whilst the others were 5th Dan. [At the time of their arrival, Kanazawa

The *dojo* inside Lyndhurst Hall, where Masters Kase, Kanazawa, Enoeda and Shirai, first attended a BKF lesson.

was thirty-three years of age, Enoeda was twenty-nine, and Shirai was twenty-seven]. Kase didn't throw his weight around of course, he didn't have to, because the 5th Dans were obviously quite subordinate to him. He'd just utter a few things and they'd run and jump. They weren't frightened of him I don't think; they respected him for his ability and seniority. I suppose what really surprised me about Master Kase was his size. He was terribly short by western standards, and I couldn't help but think, "How could a man be so good at karate and be so small?" He was built like a Sherman tank though. When I saw him perform I was totally impressed by his power. He was ever so powerful; the strongest of the group in my opinion. He was an absolute powerhouse. I think it may have been at the Upminster *dojo* that Kase performed a *fumikomi* and shattered a piece of parquet flooring. That's real power at work. I know about breaking wood, not only having broken hundreds of pieces in my time as a karateka, but also for being a carpenter. What Kase did that day was special.

"Kase was completely taken, fascinated really, with Eddie Whitcher's height. Even by western standards Eddie was tall, and broad with it, which gave you the impression that he was even bigger. Kase kept looking at Eddie, as much as to say, "How do they grow them that size?" In the end, Kase just had to find out how much strength Eddie had, and he got him up to attack *oi-zuki* to his head. Eddie charged him, and Kase just stood there in *heiko-dachi* and blocked *age-uke*. Kase's block came from the middle of his abdomen, like the old style, and not from the side as we practice today. Eddie, who was a very strong man, tried his hardest, but his arm was powered back over his head. It was amazing. We'd never seen anything like it. I was just totally shocked. I thought, "He just can't do that!" but he did, and quite a few times. It was like David and Goliath, but this David didn't need a sling!

"My first impression of Shirai was that he was the youngest in the party and technically a combination of Kanazawa and Enoeda. Kanazawa looked the all-round athlete, perfect, like a Greek god. Everything he did impressed me. I remember his *keage* – it was so fast, so high, so precise. Enoeda *Sensei* looked very powerful, very chunky, nothing was going to stop that man. If a brick wall was in his way, he'd punch it down. He didn't need a hammer. In fact, I was quite nervous of him to be honest; scared actually. I think we all were. He seemed unpredictable in those days. They were all technically excellent of course – brilliant. When Kanazawa spoke to us early on, I remember him telling us that Shirai had represented Japan in the 100 yards at the 1964 Tokyo Olympics, so he really was an outstanding athlete. All the Japanese had degrees from universities too, which was quite a rare thing in those days. Kase had studied at Senshu University, Kanazawa and Enoeda at the infamous Takushoku, and Shirai had been to Komazawa. All seemed to have great humility. They were superior men alright, make no mistake about it.

"Something else that surprised me was the width of the Japanese masters' feet. They seemed to be so wide. Kanazawa's feet were like the chocks to prevent an aircraft from moving. My son's feet are just the same, and he has to have extra wide shoes. [Michael's son, Marty, is half Japanese]. When I did freestyle, the parts of my body that always got bruised were my feet, and when I saw the Japanese feet I thought, "Oh my God! If they come at me with one of those, how I am going to stop it?" It's actually quite daunting. Those wide feet also give them good stability.

"At the Lyndhurst Hall *dojo*, later, Bell used to use a wooden table outside the *dojo* to do all the administration on. The circular table legs were turned so that thick wood was at the base of the table top and thinner wood was touching the floor. They were still fairly thick at floor level though, and Kanazawa would stand there and wedge his big toe around one side of a leg and his next toe of the same foot around the other side of the same table leg. He'd then turn his big toe around so that it touched the top of the other toe and encircled the table leg. I found that totally amazing.

"I remember one of the first things that Kanazawa *Sensei* did. I'm not completely sure whether it was on that first night or not though, but I'm pretty sure that it was. Kanazawa had, of course, lived in Hawaii for a couple of years, as I've mentioned before, and he had a reasonable command of the English language. He sat us down and spoke about using the hips in karate. We were in a circle around him, and he was standing in the middle, describing the importance of the hips, which we hadn't really considered. Before the JKA came, we didn't use our hips at all – everything was square on. We just didn't know about the use of hips and we weren't taught it either. So we punched square on and blocked square on. To illustrate the point, Kanazawa showed us how to perform a *kekomi*. He lifted his leg up and thrust his hip and leg out. I was sitting almost underneath his leg, and I saw his leg whip out at the speed of light and lock at the end. The *kime* was shattering. I thought to myself, "What am I looking at?" I knew that I was witnessing *real* karate. I was completely shocked, that's all I can say – a devastating kick. I felt confident that with such *kime* it would have killed a man. Kanazawa said that all technique comes from the hips, and he described technique, speed and power. Technique comes first, he noted, speed second, and when these are combined, you get power. This is how we must learn, he said. Try to get the correct technique, then increase speed. Of course, you had continual reassessment, because as you increase speed, technique wavers.

"Kanazawa described the different hip movements, which he said were: side on [as in *hanmi*], square on [as in *gyaku-zuki*], forward and backward [as in *mae-geri* and *ushiro-geri*], and sideward [as in *yoko-keage*]. We thought that that was very interesting. As we found out later of course, the movements Kanazawa asked us to do were not easy, especially for shoulder orientated westerners! He then performed a series of elbow strikes to Enoeda *Sensei*, first slowly, then with speed. When he did the sequence quickly, you couldn't really pick the techniques out to be honest, they were performed that quickly. It really was very impressive.

"Kanazawa continued by saying that speed was a product of correct technique and breathing. He said that you had to breathe in and out at the correct times. Breathe out as you lock a technique.

Master Kanazawa's devastating *kekomi*

Kanazawa noted that power came from the *hara*, the abdomen, when combined with speed. We found it quite complicated to be honest, because it was all new to us and we had to try to understand his pidgin English which wasn't easy. Later on, we had no trouble understanding him, but those things, acquiring the correct ear, as it were, take time.

"The other thing Kanazawa *Sensei* said was that our stances were much too high. If you look at the Pathe Pictorial film, which was made only five months before the JKA arrival, you will see what he meant.

"We all trained hard that evening to try to impress upon the Japanese masters that we were sincere students and worthy of a JKA instructor. I don't think they really instructed that night as such, but just came to watch essentially, to see what British karate was like. They wandered around, observing, and offered a few comments at the end, like the one's I've just mentioned.

"After we bowed out of the lesson, we all got changed and walked the few yards to The Admiral Napier pub in Warden Road, and had a few beers, or what have you, to get the fluid back into our bodies. That pub had a flat roof, like the Horseshoe, but I don't think it was quite so old. It had a Victorian frontage, I believe. It was built like an "L" on its side, with the living quarters sited in the vertical section. I didn't speak to any of the Japanese that evening, but they did chat to the higher grades, such as Wingrove and Jimmy Neal. Bell was having a drink too, and acting as their host. Eddie had quite a long chat with Kanazawa, but the rest of us just spoke amongst ourselves, going over what we had seen and discussing the issue of hips. It was a truly memorable evening.

"Three days later [21st April, 1965], the first demonstration ever given by the JKA in this country was held in the evening at Kensington Town Hall. Vernon Bell had arranged three such displays in his attempt to publicise JKA karate. He'd done a lot of prior advertising, with posters and so on. Bell was good at planning events like this, it was his forte, and he put a lot of hard work in. A few days later, we went to the Hornsey Town Hall [24th April, 1965], and a few days after that, to Poplar Town Hall [26th April, 1965]. The local press, and I think the national press were there, and somebody was filming. Although I took part in the very important first demonstration, I cannot recall too much about the other two. I was definitely there though, but I can't remember now, to be truthful, if I took part, after all these years. I recall that we were invited to put our karate *gi* on and take part in sample lessons, to show that British students were practising the art. Remember that karate was hardly known at all to the general public. We were on the stage at the Kensington Town Hall, and Terry Wingrove took the lesson. We just went through some basics, punches, kicks, that sort of thing, to show

how we trained. I also remember performing five-step sparring, *gohan-kumite*, and the *kata Heian Shodan* and *Heian Nidan*. They were the only *kata* I knew in any case.

"The Japanese were extremely impressive. They did some *tameshiwari* [wood breaking] and the power ... I remember that

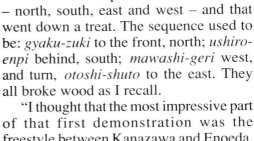

Kanazawa would perform his four breaks – north, south, east and west – and that went down a treat. The sequence used to be: *gyaku-zuki* to the front, north; *ushiro-enpi* behind, south; *mawashi-geri* west, and turn, *otoshi-shuto* to the east. They all broke wood as I recall.

"I thought that the most impressive part of that first demonstration was the freestyle between Kanazawa and Enoeda. That was really something. It was a fantastic display of exchanges. We'd never seen anything like it before. *Mae-geri* and *mawashi-geri* flying around everywhere, with deadly accuracy. It was like *dojo* freestyle, but at high speed. It wasn't about point scoring. It didn't look rehearsed, but in retrospect, I suppose it probably was, but it was rapid and it was outstanding. The Japanese performed freestyle on each of the displays. Once, Kanazawa and Shirai paired up. That was special. I suppose it went on for about thirty seconds. Time's difficult to gauge when you're absorbed. They were all exceptionally fit men.

"Kase didn't do the freestyle. He was senior, and didn't need to do it. He acted as a referee during the freestyle bouts. Kase did a self-defence demonstration though. Something that stuck in my mind, which Kase did, was to show how the *gedan-barai* was not just a block, but could be used to disengage an opponent's grip

Master Enoeda board-breaks for the cameraman backstage at the Hornsey Town Hall. Master Kase, and one other, are holding the wood.

Master Kase defends, and is in the process of countering, Master Enoeda's attack - Liverpool, April, 1965.

as well. He had one of the other Japanese instructors grip his right wrist with both hands and grasp really strongly. Remember, this was a top Japanese karate instructor gripping, and their hands are like vices. I think Kanazawa may have been clasping, now I picture it. Kase went bang, and just knocked his opponent's arms flying. It was really impressive. I couldn't see how he could do it. He was phenomenally strong. Kase could show his calibre as well, like that.

"I think they may have also performed a *kata* each, but I wouldn't have known what it was. Kase performed *kata* application as well.

Master Kanazawa performs *yoko-tobi-geri* on Mick Peachey at the Upminster *dojo* - August, 1965.

Terry Wingrove performed *Heian Sandan* on his own in front of the audience, and that looked very good. If we'd seen *Unsu* or one of the *Gojushiho*, or something similar, we wouldn't have had a clue what we were looking at.

"It was at the Hornsey Town Hall demonstration, I think, when Shirai attempted to break three or four pieces of wood, with a kick, and they wouldn't go. I remember that afterwards, around the back, he was so cross with himself, frustrated really, I suppose, that he was hitting the wall, a kind of wooden partition, quite hard actually. But it wasn't his fault, because one of the pieces of wood had a large knot in it, and he was always going to have trouble with that. Accepting the responsibility of being a representative of the JKA had its price. I suppose he felt that he had let himself and the JKA down by not making the break immediately. He was in front of a

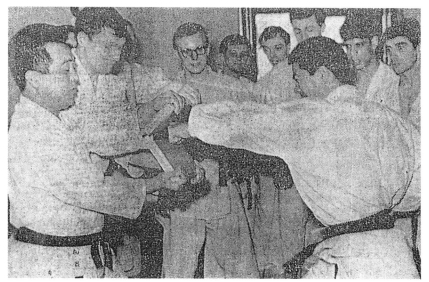

Master Kanazawa board-breaks during an unscheduled demonstration at the Upminster *dojo* – April, 1965. Master Kase and Terry Wingrove are holding the wood. Some famous Shotokan faces, to be, watch on. From right to left: Andy Sherry, Joe Chialton, Bob Poynton, Brian Harper, Jimmy Neal, Steve Cattle, unknown (possibly Rob Williams), Eddie Whitcher (whose head appears above Terry Wingrove's), and one other (possibly Roy Merrick).

very large, expectant audience, in a foreign land, that wanted to learn JKA karate, and here was an expert, a Grand Champion, who thought he could do something and failed with the first two or three attempts. To his way of thinking, it didn't look good I suppose, but of course he needn't have reproached himself. I reckon that was the kind of thing that was going through his mind. At least it showed the audience that the breaks weren't some kind of trick!

"At one or more of the demonstrations, Kanazawa I think, or it could have been Shirai, demonstrated the famous *yoko-tobi-geri*. It was the first time many of us had seen that technique performed and we thought it was spectacular. What amazing timing! I remember Kanazawa performed the side-jumping-kick on Mick Peachey at the Upminster *dojo*, and the photo was shown in the local newspaper. He never performed it on me though, I regret to say, but I was never one to jump up and volunteer.

"After the demonstrations, Vernon Bell and the JKA party went up north to Liverpool and Blackpool for a few days. When they returned to London, they stayed another couple of days and then Kase, Enoeda and Shirai went off to South Africa to teach for six months at various locations, and Kanazawa remained as the BKF instructor. He was to stay one year in the first instance, with his *honbu* [headquarters or central *dojo*] at Lyndhurst Hall, though he taught at the Kentish Town Baths one night a week as well. He was also scheduled to regularly visit the other BKF *dojo* up and down the country. It was the beginning of an extremely exciting time for British Shotokan, and for the London students in particular."

III

A WONDERFUL YEAR

Michael Randall continued: "Kanazawa taught at the Lyndhurst Hall *dojo* three evenings a week, and at the Kentish Town Baths on Friday evenings. So, I was initially training under him four times a week, and later, that became five times. Each lesson was for one and a half hours. Whatever was going I'd do the lot.

"Lyndhurst Hall was a strange place. It was like a large secondary school, but I don't think it ever was one. It may have been council offices, or something like that. The point I remember about the frontage to that building, was the vast number of windows – about two hundred, I guess. From the pavement, you walked up a flight of stone stairs, through double doors, and the main *dojo* was just down there on your left. It had a lovely light parquet wooden floor in those days, unlike the flooring in the hall used for the first visit of the Japanese, which was parquet, but much darker. That *dojo* was altogether, a far more sombre place, and to my mind completely without spirit. I didn't like that *dojo* at all. There was just something about it that didn't engage me.

"When we started training under Kanazawa, he said that he was largely going to disregard what we had done before, and start again. The initial training was then, very, very basic. Kanazawa had to take our techniques to pieces, reassemble them, and mould them into classic JKA form. The point he emphasized very strongly indeed was the use of the hips, as I mentioned before. We would always start off with warm-up exercises, then Kanazawa *Sensei* would begin with *choku-zuki*, which he called *kara-zuki*. He's the only person I've ever heard call the technique *kara-zuki*. He called this "empty-punch" because you don't use the hips. I think he did this as a deliberate ploy, to show no use of hips. He'd next get us into a low

65

zenkutsu-dachi, and we'd place our hands on our hips. We'd practise turning our hips square on, as in *gyaku-zuki* and then in *hanmi*, to count – *"ichi, ni, ichi, ni . . ."*. This would go on and on, so that the act of twisting the hips became part of us, ingrained. Our leg muscles really worked, as we tried for deeper stances with correct form. Our legs would shake under the strain. Then we'd practise the same hip movement but punching *gyaku-zuki* when our hips were square on, and blocking *tate-shuto-uke* when our hips were half-facing. Actually, that recollection isn't one hundred percent accurate, because Kanazawa didn't pull back *tate-shuto-uke*; he'd just pull back with his hand straight out, like an unturned *shuto*.

"We trained like that for years. After Kanazawa left, and I had my own *dojo*, I continued training like that. It's gruelling and demanding practice. Your whole body aches and it's easy to get bored. You'd find it hard to get away with that type of training now, as well. Modern day students just won't put up with it. They want you to do the karate for them. They have little idea of the sort of training students underwent in the early days.

"I hadn't been taught anything about breathing from either Jimmy or Terry, and Kanazawa taught us how to breathe correctly – to exhale on a technique. We would practise exhaling on the reverse-punch and then slowly inhaling as the reaction arm went out. Then, when we'd got that, we'd practise punching fast and with power, and pull back slowly. Kanazawa would complicate matters further and we'd practise *sanbon-zuki* – three techniques, but only two breaths. Again, it was, *ichi, ni, ichi, ni . . ."*, and that would go on forever too.

"We'd practise techniques slow to count, and even a punch would be broken down into two or three counts, sometimes. Then we'd move on to fast to count, then slow no count, then fast no count. Each time, twenty, thirty, even forty times. Monday and Friday sessions were the hardest. When we practised *gohon-kumite*, we also did this slow to count, fast to count, slow no count and fast no count, with probably five different partners. That's one hundred attacks and one hundred defences. Kanazawa generated an intensity in training that we hadn't really experienced before, and we always tried to excel. He pushed us so that we might. They were very demanding lessons; no question about it. Students just wouldn't stand for that type of training today, simply because they don't know the importance of what one is trying to impart to them. Wednesday and Thursday sessions were more instructional, thank goodness, because you couldn't have continued training if every lesson was like a Monday

Master Kanazawa is flanked by Michael Randall and Ray Fuller at the Kentish Town *dojo* - May to July, 1965.

or a Friday. We paid fifteen pounds, in advance, for three months training in those days.

"All our stances had to be lower. We had, really, been learning prior to the JKA arrival, Yoseikan karate, and although there were many similarities between Yoseikan and JKA karate, of that there is no doubt, Yoseikan was the "Old Shotokan." So, we had to get deeper and wider. We also had to correct our posture. Kanazawa took our karate to pieces alright. He threw the Lego set up into the air, and when it fell to the floor he reassembled the pieces and built a different type of karate. He never just walked around the *dojo* correcting, Kanazawa was always very active in the lessons.

"However, the training we'd done under Jimmy Neal, Terry Wingrove, Muramaki and Mochizuki, definitely helped. We had *kime*, but we didn't really understand it. We were also pretty supple, and we had good discipline. We certainly had the correct mental attitude towards karate, and we had tremendous stamina. We gained an enormous amount from the early BKF training, but what we lacked, essentially, was the correct method for delivering a technique, and small, but important points of form. For example, we knew how to pull our toes back for *mae-geri* and *mawashi-geri*, but we didn't know how to turn our foot for *keage* and *kekomi*. Kanazawa would teach big toe up, other toes down, foot back. Before that, we just used to turn all our toes downwards and under, to keep them out of the way. Another thing we used to do, when performing *nukite*, was to keep all the fingers as straight as possible, except for the middle finger, which we kept bent and in line with the others. Murakami taught that if you struck the eyes, the middle finger would buckle at the bridge of the nose, and the first and third fingers from the thumb would enter the eye sockets. Kanazawa said "No!" All the fingers had to be straight, as this way they would brace one another better. We were quite surprised by that, but as Kanazawa could *nukite* his way through pine boards, we reckoned he must be right!

"Back-stance was another thing. Before, we had just practised bending the back leg, but Kanazawa refined it, and said that the weight ratio was seventy percent on the back leg and thirty percent on the front leg. Back foot – toes in, knee out; front foot straight on, knee slightly forward and out. We didn't know these things then; no one in Britain did.

"*Kiba-dachi* was another stance. We'd just get into something that looked like it without really knowing what we were doing. Kanazawa said, "Toes in, knees out." Jimmy Neal just used to say, "Get lower! Get lower!" but he didn't used to say, "Get lower and do this." I used to practise *kiba-dachi* under a shelf in my mother's kitchen. I'd stand there for ten minutes or so, with the top of my head touching the underside of the shelf, so I couldn't come up. That was really good training for the legs – it really strengthened them up. My mother was pleased that I'd found something I was interested in and she didn't mind me getting in the way when she was preparing meals. She didn't know what I was really trying to do of course, but being a sickly child, she was pleased that I'd found some form of physical activity that I enjoyed. She's dead now, and karate helped me to overcome that dreadful loss.

"Eventually, after many months, and I mean many months of basics, we progressed onto combinations such as, *age-uke/gyaku-zuki, ude-uke/empi, uchi-uke/gyaku-zuki, shuto-uke/nukite, ren-geri*, and so on. The side-kicks were always performed in *kiba-dachi*. The side thrust-kick was never performed in *zenkutsu-dachi* in basics, and yet it was introduced in the front-stance during *ippon-kumite*.

"What amazes me today, is that we never had a weekly lesson set aside specifically for the practice of *kata*. Looking back, and despite what I've just said, the lessons seemed to be rather lacking in structure in a curious sort of way, but Kanazawa knew what he was doing, and he knew exactly what he wanted from us. We always started with basics. Basics, basics, basics ... *Kata* would be practised towards the end of a lesson, and we'd practise the *Heian*. We didn't practise *Taikyoku Shodan* in those days. We didn't even know that it existed, let alone that Funakoshi had devised three such forms. After the five *Heian*, we learned *Tekki Shodan*, then *Bassai-dai* and *Kanku-dai*, followed by *Enpi* and *Jitte*. If memory serves me well, that was generally the sequence Kanazawa taught the *kata* in during those days, up to black-belt. However, he also personally taught me *Hangetsu*, but I'll talk about that later.

"The training was so repetitive, so hard, that Kanazawa *Sensei* used to give us a five minute rest period half-way through the lesson, so that we could get our breath back. Believe me, we needed it. One of the things Kanazawa used to practise during this break, when we were seated, cross-legged, by the walls, was walking on his hands. He'd do a handstand at one end of the *dojo*, and off he'd go. I don't really know why he did this, to be truthful. Perhaps it was to improve his balance or to strengthen his hands and wrists? Perhaps he wanted more blood to his head? Knowing *Sensei*, it was all three, and something else besides. He never missed an opportunity to train, and that's one reason why he was so very good. Karate practice is cumulative. Kanazawa would get to the end of the *dojo* on his hands and then he would have to turn, which isn't easy when doing a handstand. The first few times he did it, he lost his balance, but he persevered and then went down the *dojo*, turned, and came back. He was practising, and if he made a mess of it he didn't bother, he just tried again. Perhaps he was showing us that he was learning something difficult too? It's the sort of thing he would have done.

"At the end of the lessons, we used to do press-ups on our knuckles, sometimes on our fingertips, and occasionally on our bent wrists, so that the backs of our hands took the weight. We'd also practice sit-ups and bunny hops, and we used to walk across the *dojo* in the bunny-hop position, on the balls of our feet, in the same way as Sumo wrestlers train.

"Most people, most students, watched Master Kanazawa for his technique. I watched him for technique too, that goes without saying, but I was primarily interested in the man. "How did he think?" "How did he tick?" I wanted to be like him. I reasoned that the personality governed the technique, and if I could work him out, then I thought the karate, as it were, would follow.

"Apart from "*Oss Sensei*", I never said a word to Kanazawa for the first few months he was with us, and he shot me down in flames the first time I did speak to him, when I asked a question. It was during one of our rest periods. I wanted to know if one should tense one's stomach muscles as one stepped forward into a forward-stance, say performing an *oi-zuki*, if one's opponent was about to kick *mae-geri*. I took the plunge, stood up, and nervously asked my question. I could hear my own heart beat. I was that anxious. I made a real muddle of it and forgot to bow, and Kanazawa picked me up immediately, and rather forcibly. "*Bow* when you speak to me!" he replied, looking daggers. Later, I realised that it was a case of the bark was worse than the bite in such situations, but it was my first question, and after building myself up to asking it, I made a mess of the whole thing and had been told off. I was so embarrassed. I went bright red. As I say, I was so shy in those days. All I said was, "*Oss Sensei! Oss Sensei!*" and bowed continuously each time I said it. I think Kanazawa realised what he'd done, and continued, "That's better," in a quiet, reasssuring voice. I sat down, wishing the earth would swallow me up, and he said to everyone that the question was a very good one, and interesting, and then he explained it.

"Kanazawa *Sensei's* first London grading for the BKF was held on the 28th July, 1965, at Lyndhurst Hall. We all had to fill out an application form for grading and a separate grading form. People find it hard to believe today, but on the application for grading form, we had to have two signed witnesses. I'm not quite sure why we had to have these witnesses, but knowing Bell, it was probably related to some other piece of paper that stated that we couldn't teach karate after grading. It all seems ridiculous today, but that was quite normal then. My first witness was Ray, and my second was a chap we called Sam Firlej, though his christian name was really Januariusz. He spoke perfect English, but I believe his father was Polish or from that part of the world – Eastern European. He was a fellow 8th kyu, and a giant of a man; very strong. We were all wary of him, because if you paired up with him there was a good chance you'd get bruised. Like Firlej, I was now going for my 7th kyu grade.

"Actually, the grading was held on two nights come to think of it – the 28th and 29th July. The grading started at 7.00 pm and everybody was required to get there early. I suppose about fifty people graded, and that was an enormous number in those days – unheard of actually. It was a very important couple of nights in the history of British Shotokan. Nobody really knew how the master intended grading us. I paid six shillings [30p] to grade that time.

"I confess to remembering virtually nothing about what I was

> *To come new life.*
> *right lost*
>
> (pa 41.)
> (pa 31.) 28/7
> GYR 583
> 28 8/65
> useld
>
> BRITISH KARATE FEDERATION.
>
> APPLICATION FORM FOR GRADING.
>
> I *Robert Eric Michael* Surname *Randall* .... Christian Names N.16
> of *3, Southwell House Boleyn rd Stoke Newington* permanent address
>
> Hereby desire to apply to compete in and be examined at the official grading
> examination at the BKF Federal dojo, Lyndhurst Hall, N.W.5. on the 28th and 29th
> July, under the supervision of Mr.Kanazawa.
>
> I have read fully, understood completely and agree to accept all the conditions
> and regulations as laid down in the official grading circular governing this
> examination. With full knowledge of the contents of this official grading
> circular, I wish to reply for the grading session to be held on Wednesday/Thursday,
> 28th/29th July at 7.00 p.m. under category A/B as set out in the grading circular.
> I agree to be present at 6.45 p.m. sharp in the main dojo, changed into Gi and to
> see that my Karate-gi is completely clean and that I am wearing the appropriate
> belt, denoting my present grade. I agree to remain until the termination of
> the grading session and then to await the result of same and I realise that under
> no circumstances may I leave early or may I arrive late whatever the
> circumstances.   I fully realise that I must be present when my name is called
> and that I will conduct myself in a quiet, dignified and correct Karate manner
> and remain alert and available for all instructions that are given, throughout
> the session.   I realise that should I not be present when my name is called,
> the examiner and/or the organising secretary, is entitled to cancel my grading.
>
> I fully understand and agree that any award given to me at the end of the
> session, neither entitles me to teach, instruct or coach Karate in any way or to
> organise a Karate group, club or branch, without the express written permission
> of the National Executive Committee of the BKF and of the technical director
> Mr.Kanazawa and only as and when decreed in the interests and requirements of
> the Federation.   Furthermore I realise that upon my promotion, my registration
> of grade with the BKF and the JKA is dependent upon all the aforegoing conditions.
> With this fully in mind I herewith enclose my BKF grading card, and postal orders
> to the value of .*6/-*..... My BKF membership Number.is.,,;;;........ My BKF
> licence is No............ and I hold ....& KYU grade ....
> awarded .... examiner ....
> Signed ..*R.Randall*..... Dated .*27.-7.-65*.......
> First witness *K.E.Fulker*......... Second witness *J.S. FIRLEJ*
> Address ...*33 BANTLEY HOUSE* Address ..*32 Tasso Road*
> ..*PHYLIS RD WATERLOO*... ........*W.G.*..............

Michael's application to take part in Kanazawa's first London grading.

asked to do, technically, at that grading. We performed *kihon, kumite*
and *kata*, and it would have been much the same as a JKA grading
today, though possibly more basic, as we were in a transitional period.
We were required to stay to the end and the results were then given.

"As it turned out, everybody passed something. One or two
students stayed on their existing grades, as I recall. It was unfortunate,
but Jimmy Neal, who was a 1st kyu under Murakami, was demoted
to 2nd kyu. That must have been very hard for him, being our past
teacher, but he was still the senior grade in the class. He was the

JAPAN KARATE ASSOCIATION.
(INCORPORATE BY CHARTER IN JAPAN)

GRADING APPLICATION

CLUB .B..K.F..................

SURNAME RANDALL............   FIRST NAME(S) ROBERT. ERIC. MICHHEL

ADDRESS 2, SOUTHWELL. HOUSE   DATE OF BIRTH ..8:4..1944:....
DOLEYN..ROAD...N:16.....

PREVIOUS KARATE EXPERIENCE ....1 YEAR..7.MONTHS

OCCUPATION CARPENTER....

EXAMINERS NAME ....

PRESENT GRADE	BASIC	FORM	KUMITE	TOTAL	RESULT	EXAMINERS REMARKS
8th KYU	5 •	5 •	5 •	80	5 KYU	
	集中を順練直でまる力に枝が葉					

EXAMINATION FEE — PAID   DATE OF EXAMINATION ....

AMOUNT RETURNED ☐

4th KYU & UNDER = 4/-

3rd KYU & ABOVE = 10/-. IF EXAMINEE OF 3rd KYU & ABOVE FAILS
THE GRADING, THE SUM OF 6/- WILL BE
RETURNED.

SHODAN = £2. 0.0.   ON FAILING £1.10.0. RETURNED

NI-DAN = £2.10.0.   ON FAILING £2. 0.0. RETURNED

SAN-DAN = £3. 0.0.   ON FAILING £2.10.0. RETURNED

CERTIFICATES OF PROFICIENCY OF THE J.K.A. ARE AWARDED TO ALL GRADES
ABOVE 3rd KYU.

BMF 583 28/8/65 u.fill
GR

Michael's first grading application form, under Kanazawa, when he was
awarded 5th kyu.

only one. Wingrove had got married and gone to South Africa a few weeks before the grading. He went on to get a JKA black-belt from Shirai whilst out there, before he went to Japan. A number of people jumped grades. I went to 5th kyu and wore a purple belt, along with Peter Labasci and Mick Peachey. I got a total of eighty points – out of one hundred, I suppose? I received good marks on *kihon, kata* and *kumite*. On the grading form, *kihon* was not actually written, "basic" was, and for *kata*, "form", was written. I didn't do a 7th kyu, 6th kyu and a 5th kyu grading though. Because of the nature of the event, seniority and expertise, and so on, that was where I was ranked at this time by JKA standards. I can't even remember which *kata* I performed for the grading. I hadn't graded for a year, nor had anyone else who started around the time Ray and I did, but it showed that the Murakami based training under Neal and Wingrove had been very good, because we had had less than three months of training under Kanazawa.

"I remember the grades the other students I knew, received too. Nick and Chris Adamou were ranked 7th kyu, as was John Goodbody, a journalist. Goodbody was a very strong man, built like a bodybuilder, but not that supple, as I recall. I can't say that I particularly liked him. Pauline, Jack Johnson and Sam Firlej made 6th kyu. Old Arthur Nightingale and Lassey became temporary 5th kyu. Ray did very well, and was awarded a temporary 4th kyu, along with Harper and Merrick. John Chisholm received 3rd kyu as did Eddie, Rob Williams, and one other [Harry Peters]. Yes, I recall those gradings results with great clarity, because they were deemed so important at the time."

Nick Adamou recalled an incident that occured shortly after this grading that gives a very good insight into Michael Randall's character: "[I asked] ... Mick how he managed to accelerate so incredibly quickly when he performed *oi-zuki*. His first reaction was to instantly humble himself and mention how slow and imperfect his *oi-zuki* was in comparison with Kanazawa *Sensei's*. He then went on to say that his *oi-zuki* wasn't so wonderful anyway, because his balance wasn't that good. It was amazing and very uplifting that someone's whose karate, even then, was so very good, should have made such a big effort not to allow me to put him on a pedestal, that he thought he didn't deserve. His philosophy seemed to be to honestly look at all his weak points and anything that was left over might deserve some praise. Anyway, after he had related all that he thought was not good about his lunge-punch, he then went on to explain how he trained on his *oi-zuki* in order to improve it. He said that just as in a *kiba-dachi*, when one contracts the inside muscles of the legs together in order to move across when performing a side-kick, so this is what he practised in order to assist in the pulling up of the back leg to the front leg when stepping forward in a *zenkutsu-dachi*. I remember at the time thinking to myself that I had learned two things from him, as I hadn't realised the point regarding the *kiba-dachi*."

Michael Randall continued: "A month after the grading, Kanazawa held a week long course at Grange Farm, a residential centre, in Chigwell, exactly as Murakami had done the year before. I don't remember much about the course believe it or not, but I did attend. Immediately afterwards, Kanazawa held another week course up at Lilleshall, in Shropshire, but I wasn't able to go to that because of work and family commitments, though some of the lads did, including the Adamou brothers.

"Ray and I used to get to the *dojo* early to loosen up, and one day we arrived at the same time as Kanazawa. This was at the Kentish Town Baths and there were only the three of us there. Kanazawa called us over and he had this little egg shaped container, about an inch in height, which he carefully took out of his pocket and showed us. We looked on interestingly, but thought nothing special about it, and then Kanazawa opened it, and out popped this phallus on a spring like a Jack-in-the-box. Ray and I just fell about laughing on the floor, and as we did so, this tiny penis bobbed up and down on the end of the spring. *Sensei* looked at us strangely and didn't laugh. It wasn't a joke to him at all. He was deadly serious. Realising this, Ray and I tried to gain our composure, but it was no good, and we just couldn't stop laughing. I can see that little penis now, wobbling about! Apparently, it was a kind of fertility symbol. Perhaps someone gave it to him, I don't know, but I won't forget that incident for as long as I live.

"I recall another interesting incident from the Kentish Town Baths. Kanazawa had his own banner, or flag, that he'd been awarded by the JKA. His name was on it. I think that it was bestowed upon him for winning three JKA titles. He really treasured that. It was multi-coloured, with gold and silver too, and he showed it to us one Friday evening after training.

"Kanazawa would tell us all sorts of stories. I remember one, in particular, about Master Funakoshi. Kanazawa was at Takushoku University – he changed to that university from another university in

The flag that was presented to Master Kanazawa for winning three JKA titles – 1965.

his first year, so that he could train in karate – and he was asked to pick Funakoshi *Sensei* up in a taxi and bring him to the university *dojo*. Kanazawa said that whilst in the taxi with Funakoshi, he wondered whether this frail, old man, who appeared to rely on a walking stick, was really any good at karate, and whether he could even block an attack. As he was thinking this, Funakoshi said, "You can try if you like!" Kanazawa *Sensei* told us that he would never forget that incident. I could see by his face that Kanazawa was full of admiration for Funakoshi, and he called him a great master.

"Another little anecdote, which is similar to the above, was when Kanazawa, Mick Peachey and I went down to Plymouth by train. The BKF Plymouth *dojo* [Plymouth Bushido Karate Club] was run by a chap called Herrity. If I remember correctly, the *dojo* was based in Pennycross [22, Fountains Crescent, to be exact]. We used to stay at the instructor's house. The three of us were in a compartment on our way down to Devon, and Kanazawa was sitting on one side, Mick and I were on the other side. *Sensei* was in a deep sleep, and he deliberately moved a foot and placed it on top of Mick's feet, which were crossed in front of him and opposite to Kanazawa. Mick looked at me in a strange, not to say worried way, and I asked him what the matter was. "Well, I was wondering whether I could kick him now,"

Mick said to me, "and just as I was thinking that, *Sensei's* foot came over and rested on mine!" It's quite true.

"There's another little story that happened on a train, this time to Portsmouth. Mick Peachey and I would go down to teach at that *dojo* for Kanazawa, and we'd seen this "hat-kick" in a book. There was a picture of a man wearing a large, ten-gallon hat and he was kicking it off his own head. It sounds stupid today, totally contrived, but we took it all very seriously then. Mick and I would stand in the corridor of the train and we'd put a biro in our mouths for the other to kick out with *mae-geri*. We never missed an opportunity to practice! Anyway, we became very good at this, but one day, just as Mick kicked, the train jolted, and he kicked me under the chin. That might sound painful, but I had my tongue slightly out at the time. I could have cried with the pain, and the blood ... Luckily, it wasn't a full *mae-geri* or he'd have broken my neck."

Another, "not so sensible" incident, concerning a certain misplaced enthusiasm, that involved Michael Randall around this time is told in a short story by Nick Adamou: "[A group of us] ... including Mick Randall, were walking back from an event ... Mick was a brown-belt, I think, and I was a purple-belt. It was about 11.30 pm, and every time we attempted to hail a bus, it just flew past. We continued walking and then we saw another bus coming towards us at great speed. It was a Green Line bus, and the bus stop seemed to be the sort that accepted these buses. However, it was speeding up, and obviously wasn't going to stop. Instead of putting his hand out to halt the bus, Mick thrust his leg and foot out in the form of a perfectly executed *yoko-geri-kekomi*. There was a bit of a problem with distancing though, and Mick's foot hit the bus with a great thud [denting it]!"

Michael continued: "I remember that one Japanese *sensei* told us about Master Masatoshi Nakayama, the Chief Instructor to the JKA, who first visited Great Britain a few years later. This *sensei* said that Nakayama was not frightened of anyone or anything, bar one exception. Apparently, Nakayama was petrified of snakes. When Nakayama saw a snake, he froze, pointed, and said, "Get rid of it! Get rid of it!" or words to that effect.

"I suppose everyone is wary, if not frightened, of something. I don't like insects, and spiders in particular. I really don't like them and I'd suppose you'd say that I've got a phobia – arachnophobia. [The morbid fear of snakes is ophiophobia]. I don't like flying either, like another famous Japanese instructor. Both of us get a dreadful sickening feeling in the stomach, but I can overcome that.

"In October of 1965, Kanazawa took a month off and visited Kase, Enoeda and Shirai in South Africa. He left teaching instructions for the senior grades, such as Jimmy Neal, Eddie, Rob Williams and Chisholm, who taught in his absence. The lessons were interesting of course, but it just wasn't the same and we all just bided our time until *Sensei* returned.

"The group of London brown-belts always covered for Kanazawa when he was away teaching at other BKF *dojo*, such as at Liverpool, Blackpool, Bradford, York, Nottingham, Dundee and Aberdeen. On one rainy evening in October that year, at Lyndhurst Hall, I found myself, a 5th kyu, to be the senior grade at the *dojo*, and was left with no option really than to take the lesson. We got underway, stretching, and guess who walked in – Vernon Bell. As I've mentioned before, I was very wary of Bell, I don't mind admitting it – a lot of us were. He had an aura about him – strange and eccentric. We knew he was a good judoka and a 2nd Dan in karate, though, as I've noted, I never once saw him train. But the way he spoke down to you and the way he treated you, left you feeling inadequate and in some considerable unease. Well, it did me anyway. He was also a lot older than us and an accomplished hypnotist, which was very unnerving if you didn't know anything about the subject – and I didn't! I remember being very anxious when he walked into the *dojo*, with that air around him, finding me teaching at his club without his permission. Much to my relief, he said I'd acted correctly, and left, and I continued for the evening. However, it took me some time to quieten down and get back into my stride.

"Although I was very nervous of Bell in those days, he was a just and honest man. It was simply that he was so very direct and abrupt, and didn't suffer fools gladly. If anyone was coming out with any rubbish, he'd tell them straight away and in no uncertain terms. Although we thought he was very odd, he was a man to be admired and respected. After all, he was the first British karate black-belt; had introduced karate to Great Britain; formed the BKF; and, had organized for the JKA to come over. I remember that on one occasion, Bell brought one of his sons up to either Lyndhurst Hall or the Kentish Town Baths and, after karate practice, a training friend and I, whose name I can't recall, joined the two of them for a Chinese meal at a restaurant in Finsbury Park. So, I don't want to create the wrong impression, for we were all on friendly terms.

"My next grading was on the 8th November, 1965, and I graded to 4th kyu. Again, I got a total of eighty points. Kanazawa judged my basics to be average, the *kata* good, but I was marked down on the sparring. I remember that the grading fee had gone up to ten shillings [50p]. I was living at 88, Lordship Park, Stoke Newington, with my wife. Her illness was upon her and continued, cruelly. Still now, more than thirty years on, she has to go to hospital. A terrible business; poor woman. She really paid the price for bringing new life into this world.

"Peter Lebasci and Merrick received 4th kyu as well. I don't think Mick Peachey graded, though I forget the reason why. Ray was awarded his 3rd kyu, and Eddie, Rob and Chisholm became 2nd kyu, and wore the white strip along the belt. Jimmy Neal didn't grade. It was on this occasion that Will Mannion graded [to 8th kyu]. Will became my student, and is the most senior of all my students, in terms of date started, still practising, though I regret to say that he no longer trains with me.

"Kanazawa had a large collection of photgraphs of himself at the JKA. They'd be like gold dust today. You should have seen them – fantastic. Quite a few of these were out of Nakayama's *Dynamic Karate*, which had yet to be published in the west. There were a number showing muscle tension with Kanazawa wearing boxer shorts. He had an incredible karate musculature. He was like a living anatomy lesson. A lot of the photos were quite small though. I remember that he showed us a tremendous photograph of himself actually winning the JKA *kumite* title in 1957, with a broken hand. The photographer snapped the shot just as Kanazawa was scoring his winning point – marvellous. I've never seen it published. As his opponent was performing a *mawashi-geri*, Kanazawa stepped in and put his leg behind the supporting leg of the kicker, and threw him. The story, as Kanazawa told it, was that his opponent, Katsunori Tsuyama, had a wonderful *mawashi-geri*, which was so fast it couldn't be beaten. Kanazawa thought, "How can I avoid such a kick?" On top of that, he had his broken hand, an injury sustained a few days before, which meant that he was naturally extremely wary of blocking on that side. He realised that he would have to adopt a different strategy if he was to stand a chance. He told us that he wasn't actually going to enter for the final bout originally, but his mother insisted that he must. So, the dilemma of how to overcome this invincible kick was naturally of primary consideration. He reasoned that if he kept close to Tsuyama and rushed forward as the inevitable *mawashi-geri* began, he wouldn't have to block it, because the kick would go

JAPAN KARATE ASSOCIATION.

(Incorporate by Charter in Japan)

GRADING APPLICATION.

CLUB...B.K.F.......................

SURNAME...RANDALL............ FIRST NAME(S)...ROBERT.MICHAEL.....

ADDRESS 88, LORDSHIP PARK,... DATE OF BIRTH..8.4.44.......
STOKE NEWINGTON. N.16.

PREVIOUS KARATE EXPERIENCE..1 year. 11 months.

OCCUPATION. CARPENTER.......

EXAMINERS NAME E. No1D14. KANAZAWA

PRESENT GRADE	BASIC	FORM	KUMITE	TOTAL	RESULT	EXAMINERS REMARKS
5 KYU	40	4	4	80	4 KYU	不日同 多本情

EXAMINATION FEE [10] per Utell. DATE OF EXAMINATION 8./11./65...

AMOUNT RETURNED [ ]

4th KYU & UNDER = 4/-.

3rd KYU & ABOVE = 10/-. IF EXAMINEE OF 3rd KYU & ABOVE FAILS
THE GRADING, THE SUM OF 6/- WILL BE
RETURNED.

SHODAN = £2. 0.0. ON FAILING £1.10.0. RETURNED

NI-DAN = £2.10.0. ON FAILING £2. 0.0. RETURNED

SAN-DAN = £3. 0.0. ON FAILING £2.10.0. RETURNED

CERTIFICATES OF PROFICIENCY OF THE J.K.A. ARE AWARDED TO ALL GRADES
ABOVE 3rd KYU.

Entered BKF Grady Registry 717 (BKF) /65 Utell.
C/c lost- New licence issued
357/11/65

49.

Michael's second grading application form, under Kanazawa, when he was
awarded 4th kyu.

past him. And that's what he did. It was a brilliant photograph. Later, I studied photography, and I would have been proud to have taken that shot.

"As an aside, a few years on, I took a photo of Kanazawa *Sensei* performing *yoko-tobi-geri* at my Winchmore Hill *dojo*. I developed and printed it myself, at home, in my own little darkroom. I sent the photo up to *Amateur Photographer* magazine and was awarded a certificate of merit.

"Anyway, Kanazawa carried a kind of small, dark coloured rucksack, with a zip, navy blue I think it was, with him, and he kept these photographs in there. One day, he came to the *dojo* and said that he'd lost the rucksack – left it on a train. He was so casual about it, as though it didn't matter. We were totally amazed that it just didn't seem to bother him – the fact that he'd lost this wonderful collection. We said, "*Sensei! Sensei!* what train?" We were in an absolute panic. In fact, the photos were eventually recovered, because they were just left on the train and the guard found them. But it was the way that he dismissed those photographs as irrelevant. We were beginning to understand that his values were different from most peoples'. He only really thought about karate and the pictures were a by-product; they didn't matter.

"Kanazawa was not a Christian. I don't think he was a Buddhist either. When we asked him about religion, he was always a bit cagey. I think he believed in Shinto, the forces of nature and the powers about us. Karate was basically his religion. I remember someone once asked Kase what his religion was, and he said that it was karate. Karate-Do is a Way, and is a religion to people who truly follow its path. If you asked Kanazawa *Sensei* about deep matters, he always harked back to karate. He saw the world through his art. A lot of Japanese are like that. They are very eclectic, taking bits from here and bits from there. They're a very practical people. If something doesn't work, doesn't help them, they discard it. They're not dogmatic.

"Another little story I recall during this period concerned an old Japanese man, Mr. Michigu, who owned a Japanese shop in South Kensington, near the tube station. It was the only Japanese shop that I was aware of in London at the time. Michigu sold the JKA karate *gi*. I remember on one occasion going to the shop with Kanazawa *Sensei*, and I was quite astonished to hear Kanazawa call Mr. Michigu, "*sensei*." The first question I asked myself was, "What Dan grade must this old boy hold?" I didn't realise then, that old people were

On the steps of Eros, Piccadilly - November, 1965, to February, 1966. From back to front, left to right: Nick Adamou, 6th kyu; Martin Bayliss; Chris Adamou, 6th kyu; Mick Peachey, 5th kyu; Michael Randall, 4th kyu; Master Kanazawa.

highly respected, revered even, for their age, in Japan. Mister Michigu must have been about eighty I suppose, maybe even older, and was very small and frail, just like his wife. Kanazawa looked up to him for his many years of experience of life and his acquired knowledge. Michigu was terribly proud that Kanazawa called him *sensei*, and on a subsequent visit I remember him telling me that Kanazawa was his son. I thought he really was his son; I really believed it. I remember Michigu saying, "My son" and doing a kick at the same time, but of course he couldn't kick. He wore these straw slippers and as he kicked, one flew off and hit the ceiling. I mentioned the "my son" incident to Kanazawa and he explained it to me.

"On another occasion, a certain lady student went to buy a karate *gi* at Michigu's shop. She telephoned and he said that he had plenty of karate *gi* in stock. When she got there, Mr. Michigu said he hadn't got any. Later on, I realised that – I don't know if it was because he was so old, or because he thought that women shouldn't do karate – that you had to treat him in a very traditional fashion. You had to go in and say, "How are you? It's nice to see you," comment on his shop, and so on. He wouldn't sell you anything unless he liked you. You had to meet his approval as a person before he would sell you anything. The selling was secondary to the fact that the person buying his goods had to be worthy of buying the goods from him.

"Talking about karate *gi*, there was a phase when everybody wanted their names written in Japanese on the left breast of their karate *gi*. I acquired some laundry ink and a paint brush and went up to *Sensei* in the changing rooms and asked if he would do it for me. He said that he would. British names don't translate exactly, and mine was "Mr. Randori." When people saw that, I was quite pleased, because *randori* means freestyle in judo. I thought that it was nice that my name had something to do with a martial art, because it could have said anything. Kanazawa obliged a lot of people this way. Some time later, Kase visited the *dojo* and was looking at our karate *gi* and pronouncing the names. When he came to Ray Fuller's, Kase went, "Ohhhhhh!" and called Kanazawa over, and started having a go at him. We found out later that Kanazawa *Sensei* had written on Ray's karate *gi*, "naked women", because Ray had an eye for the girls every minute. All we wanted to do was karate and didn't have much time for the girls, but Ray was chasing them all he could. The incident might sound a bit as though Kanazawa was stepping on sacred ground by doing that, but it's not so really, for the Japanese have got a wicked sense of humour.

Mae-geri on the steps of Eros. Left to right: Martin Bayliss, Mick Peachey, Nick Adamou, Master Kanazawa, Michael Randall, Chris Adamou.

Master Kanazawa counters *ushiro-geri* to Michael Randall on the steps of Eros, before dealing with Mick Peachey.

"Another time, Enoeda *Sensei* came down to Lyndhurst Hall, shortly after being posted to Liverpool. It was around Christmas, 1965, anyway. He'd occasionally come down to see Kanazawa. At the end of the lesson, the two instructors decided they would do some freestyle with us. I think it was with a view to seeing what standard we were up to in freestyle, though we never practised it in the *dojo* at all. I didn't understand why we had to do it, if we'd never done it. I once asked Kanazawa *Sensei* about freestyle, and he said there was no need for it. He said that we had to practice basics and *jiyu-ippon* and that the freestyle would then come quite naturally from it. Even today, I don't believe this is so, but that is what he said at the time.

"We all had a little go, and Kanazawa and Enoeda toyed with us. We were all scared stiff to be honest. I was petrified. We had seen what they could really do, but we tentatively did our best. There I was, a humble purple-belt, facing JKA champions! We couldn't score on them of course, but Eddie did, by accident! Eddie was a 2nd kyu at the time, and was having his little go with Kanazawa. Kanazawa just played around with him really. Then Enoeda called out *Yame*. Just at that moment, when Kanazawa stopped, relaxed his attention,

Eddie caught him with a headbutt. Now I know that Eddie used to say that he caught him with a punch to the lower lip, but I saw it, and I'm sure it was a headbutt. They were grappling a bit at the time, and *Sensei* was having a bit of fun showing that he could throw him. They were very close and Eddie accidentally brought his head down on Kanazawa's mouth after Enoeda called "Stop." It was no big deal really, as they say, and *Sensei* didn't seem troubled by it at all. We all knew that Eddie wouldn't have done it deliberately – just one look at his facial expression told you that – and we also knew perfectly well that Kanazawa could have flattened him quite easily if he'd wanted to. Then it was Eddie's turn to pair up with Enoeda. Eddie received a superb *mawashi-geri* to the side of his head. I saw it, and it was lightning fast. The *mawashi* came up and smacked Eddie – Bang! and he went sprawling. Actually, he flew backwards onto the floor, rolled, and ended up near the door. His legs went up into the air and lodged through the wall bars. He was lying on his back with his legs above him locked into the bars. It was really weird, and it frightened the life out of us. I thought, "My God!" It was devastating. Enoeda's freestyle was second to none really. That shut us all up, and it taught Eddie a lesson he'd never forget. After that we became very wary of Enoeda – you know, "Don't upset that man!"

"I lived karate then, as I do now. I used to wake up in the morning, jump out of bed, and turn the light switch on with the ball of my foot -*mawashi-geri* or *mae-geri*. At work, in the lifts, I used to select the floor I wanted to go to with my toes. I wanted a kick like Enoeda's! Everything was practising. Every spare moment I had at work I'd try breaking wood, that kind of thing. Being a carpenter, I had access to an almost unlimited supply of wood. I mainly used to practise *shuto* or *tetsui*.

"It's funny the things one remembers. I recall going to visit *Sensei* at his flat off the Finchley Road, along with Mick Peachey and the Adamou brothers. We used to train every free moment. As Kanazawa wasn't there, we found a little side road and trained in the street. We found a wall, and we took it in turns to practise *kiba-dachi* on it, moving along the wall with cross-over stances. That's the sort of thing we used to do. We lived, ate, and slept karate. I remember that very strongly."

As it turned out, Nick Adamou recalled the incident as well: "On some occasions, Kanazawa *Sensei* would invite all of us around to his flat for discussions on karate, and after, we would go out for a Chinese meal. These occasions were jewels, and we spent the whole

Master Kanazawa counters with a *jodan mawashi-geri* to Eddie Whitcher's *oi-zuki* - Lyndhurst Hall, 1965.

day in a state of joy and anticipation when one of these meetings had been arranged. As the moment arrived, and after having all met up at Finchley Road Station, we were devastated to find a small piece of paper stuck to Kanazawa's front door, on which were written three crushing words, "Gone to Belgium." At that time, Mick had been reading books on Zen Buddhism, as I had, and many times we used to comment, hilariously, on some of the very strange things that enlightened Zen masters would do in order to shock their students into enlightenment. When I, along with the rest of the group read the message, and fell into the depths of depression, Mick started to laugh quietly, and began stroking the ridge between his eyebrows and the top of his nose. In a mixture of feelings and expressions encompassing melancholy, seriousness, and the underlying possibility of hysterical humour, Mick quietly compared the whole situation to one of his Zen stories. From gloom and despair, we were collapsing on the floor with laughter...

"Mick, along with the rest of us, decided to go through all the *kihon-ippon-kumite* that we had been taught by Kanazawa *Sensei*, and I remember Mick telling me that he had heard from such and such a person that in Japan, when some students pass their black-belts, they put themselves through certain tests in order to test their proficiency. One of these tests was to perform all the kicks from the top of a narrow wall. Fifteen minutes later, we were all queuing up beside the chosen wall on a road just off Finchley Road High Street, whilst Mick attempted numerous *mae-geri, keage, kekomi* and *mawashi-geri*. This escalated into all of us attempting one-step sparring on the wall, and was only finally brought to a halt when a police patrol car drove by and, keeping its window very largely shut, asked us to move along."

Michael, taking up the theme of spiritual enlightenment, tells a funny story about three, here un-named, Japanese *Sensei*, referred to as S1, S2 and S3. Michael recalled: "We were in someone's flat, perhaps a year or so later, having a drink and a chat about spiritual matters, which most of us were interested in. We'd all had a few too many drinks. Believe me, some of the Japanese can certainly knock back the booze, and they really like the whisky. We were all sitting down, and one of the students asked S1, the senior instructor present, whether he had a third eye. The third eye is a kind of all knowing awareness. S1 said that he had, so the student turned and asked S2, the next in rank, whether he too had a third eye. S2 also replied that he had. So then, the student asked S3, the junior instructor present, whether he had a third eye. Now the three Japanese spoke at this point, and it was decided, for some reason, that S3 couldn't have a third eye. Grumpily, S3 stood up and walked out of the room in a rather unsteady fashion, and a couple of us followed him. Anyway, S3 opened the back door for a breath of fresh air, and took a few steps out onto the patio. As he did this he said, in a rather slurred fashion, away from S1 and S2, "I too have got third eye!" The hilarious thing was that as he proclaimed this, as he confidently told us that he was all knowing, all seeing, he fell over the dustbins!"

"I recall something about one of Kanazawa's flats. Kanazawa had three different flats in quite a short time. The first was in Compayne Gardens as I recall, and the other two were off the Finchley Road and Edgware Road, I think. The Compayne Gardens flat was a basement flat, because I remember having to go down a flight of steps to knock on the door. It was a dark and fairly sombre place, but it was okay. Bell acquired it for Kanazawa. It was self-contained, with a kitchen, toilet and bathroom, bedroom and lounge. His wardrobe was a length of string tied from his bed to a chair.

"Although I started with Ray Fuller, I got friendly and tended to associate more with people like Mick Peachey and the Adamou brothers. All the time Eddie Whitcher was there. I thought the world of that man, and I felt a very great personal sadness, a tremendous loss, when he died [of cancer in 1990]. He was a great man. A real karateka and not like the self-proclaimed rubbish you get today. Mick and I were real pals, and because Eddie and Mick lived close to one another over Romford way, they became friends as well. Mick Peachey and I followed *Sensei* around the most. I think I can say that. Later, Jack Johnson came along. Ray never had that much to do with *Sensei* in the sense that he didn't go and knock on his door all the time, like we did. Although Ray held the Japanese in high esteem for their ability, he thought that we were subserviant, and he didn't like that. He was happy to bow of course and say, "*Oss Sensei*", to the Japanese instructors, to give them their due, but he wasn't going to ingratiate himself, which was fair enough. I'm sure he thought we were making the *Sensei* too important. We were trying to take over the role of being Japanese students you see. We wanted to learn and be as good to the Japanese *Sensei* as we could, and to give them the respect that we thought they should have. In particular, we were Kanazawa *Sensei's* satellites, and our lives revolved around him.

"I recall something that we thought was very unusual, at least initially, about Kanazawa at that time. We never used tissues in those

Master Kanazawa performs a 'special' technique upon Mick Peachey – Lyndhurst Hall, 1966.

days, and everybody used handkerchiefs. We could never understand why Kanazawa *Sensei* would get a piece of paper out of his pocket and blow his nose on it. We couldn't understand it, and actually were totally disgusted, to be honest. One day we asked him about it, and said that it was dirty. He replied that it wasn't dirty at all. He said, "Why English people blow their nose and put the handkerchief back in their pocket and keep it in there for days, with all those germs on?" When we thought about it, we realised that Kanazawa was right, and it's one of the dirtiest habits in the world!

"Another thing about hygiene that we didn't understand, was about going to the loo. The Japanese work a different system to us. We go to the loo [urinate] and wash our hands after, as much as to say that touching your private parts is dirty. In fact, if you're like the Japanese and bathe once a day, you're perfectly clean. What is logical to the Japanese is that if you are clean down there, as it were, and your hands are dirty, it's better by far to wash your hands *before* you go to the loo. What do you want to touch yourself for if your hands are filthy from touching communial hand-rails, door handles, and so on? The hands are germ laden. So we watched *Sensei* wash his hands first and then go to the loo. We thought, "What does it mean? It doesn't make any sense." Later on, we asked him about that too, and he explained it. The Japanese are so hygienic, but they get their hygiene the right way round.

"Because Kanazawa didn't have a very good command of the English language, if he didn't understand anything I said, he used to say, "Oh Mr. Randly! What meaning? What meaning?" [Kanazawa would pronounce Randall as "Randly"]. I'm sure that he thought that some of the things that British people did too, were "What meaning?" as well.

"Talking of language difficulties, I remember a funny story involving Kanazawa. One of the students at the club, an old chap, or he seemed old at the time, probably about fifty, asked *Sensei* if he liked walking. Kanazawa replied that he did, that he liked it very much, so the student said that he'd take him on a walk, and *Sensei* agreed. The student said that he'd pick him up and take him for a walk across the fields or something. Well, what Kanazawa didn't know was that this chap was a fell walker, a really seasoned hiker, almost a professional, and when we saw Kanazawa *Sensei* at the next lesson, he seemed really quite tired. Well, he would have been, because in walking you emphasise different muscles from karate. I think the student had taken him on a proper hike of twenty odd miles, over rivers, up and down mountains and the like. *Sensei* said that he'd been taken miles and miles. He was really fed up. He didn't like that one. We all thought that it was hilarious.

"It may have been later on, but the Japanese love to stop and watch something unusual going on. We were driving down Camden High Road, I believe, and there was this enormous fire. Kanazawa said, "Oh stop! Stop! I want to watch fire." We said *"Oss Sensei*, it's

Master Kanazawa performs an *ashi-barai* upon Mick Peachey – Lyndhurst Hall, 1966.

only a fire." He turned to me and said, "Japanese like watching." They're mesmorised by unusual things.

"At the beginning of 1966, I remember a series of spectacular breaks that Enoeda and Kanazawa did for Bernard Braden on the *Braden Beat*. I went along with Mick Peachey, Eddie Whitcher and the Adamou brothers, to each event. It happened three times, and we were all on television wearing our karate *gi*.

"What happened was that Braden had challenged a certain Japanese karate instructor to come along to break a very thick plank of obeche wood. The instructor didn't turn up apparently, and Kanazawa and Enoeda went along to see if they could do it. The whole story is reported in detail in *Shotokan Dawn*, and I don't want to repeat it here for it is comprehensively told there, but essentially what happened was that Enoeda broke a four inch section of the wood live on television, and Braden received a number of phone calls or letters saying that it was a fluke, wood four inches thick cannot be broken by a punch. Braden invited the two *sensei* back and Kanazawa performed a north, south, east and west series of breaks, against the same wood. However, this time the wood was waterlogged, and impossible for a human being to break. I just didn't see how he was going to do it. We all took up our positions though, holding the wood; the cameras rolled, and Kanazawa went through a slow rehearsal. I don't recall which piece I was holding, but I think it was the piece he punched *gyaku-zuki*. To cut a very eventful story short, he broke all four pieces – a punch, front-kick, side elbow and knife-hand. I couldn't believe he'd done it to be honest. That must rank as one of the greatest *tameshiwari* displays ever given, anywhere. I remember taking a piece of that obeche wood back to the carpenters at work, and showing them. I think I mentioned that we were going to be on television and they watched the programme. They were amazed when they saw the thickness of the wood. The knuckle indentations were cleary visible, where Kanazawa had punched it. I wished I'd kept that piece of wood, I really do, but I didn't think of it at the time. That was a truly incredible series of breaks and I am personally very proud to have been associated with them.

"The blinds were amazing too. There was a certain make of Venitian blind that the manufacturers said couldn't be broken, or something like that. They were new, and made of aluminium, rather than the traditional wooden slats. This was after the *Braden Beat* wood-breaking episode, and the manufacturers advert showed the back of a karate man with a caption like, "Even he can't break them!" The manufacturers or advertisers had obviously seen *Sensei's* impressive breaks on television, and had reasoned that peoples' imaginations had been inspired by the topic and would buy the blinds through this advert, because they suggested that they were unbreakable. Someone from the *Braden Beat* came down to the *dojo* and asked Kanazawa if he could break them, and Kanazawa said that he'd try. The blinds were hanging on a kind of scaffolding in the studio. I was on one side, supporting the structure, and Mick Peachey was on the other side. Kanazawa was in the middle, facing the blinds, with his back to the camera, just as in the advert. Kanazawa powered through the blinds as if they were matchsticks with a downward *shuto*. The funny thing about this, at least from my point of view, was as Kanazawa went through the blinds I pulled a face [a kind of amazed and gormless gaze], looking through the hole Kanazawa had created. I just stood there staring with this stupid expression on my face, and then realized that I was looking straight into the camera! When it was broadcasted, you saw Kanazawa's back and his *shuto*

Masters Kanazawa and Enoeda give a karate demonstration on television, whilst Eddie Whitcher and Jasper Lassey look on – 1966.

Note the thickness of the obeche wood, to be broken, by Lassey's feet.

powering through the blinds, and then you see this face – like an idiot, like an absolute moron. What made the episode worse for me, was that they showed it more than once. I suppose it added to the whole thing though, in the sense that audiences would have thought, "Look! He's amazed too!" but I don't want to see that clip again, thank you very much!

"Kanazawa had tremendous power. I remember when Ray Fuller brought a hand-held *makiwara* to Lyndhurst Hall. Either he, or I, had made it at work, and we asked Kanazawa whether he'd like to try it. He placed the *makiwara* against the infamous wall bars and struck it. The whole *dojo* vibrated with the power of the punch. Later, I had a little business making *makiwara*.

"Kanazawa never seemed to get any real injuries, and he used the Salonpas medicated plasters if he ever had a stiff joint, sprain or bruise. [It is recorded that Kanazawa consulted an osteopath on the 3rd May, 1965, at a cost of three pounds]. You can get them today. You peel the back off – a kind of clear plastic – and the plasters are sticky, because they are impregnated with a medication, which seems to draw the injury out somehow and relieve the pain. I use them even to this day, and have found them to be excellent. They contain menthol and camphor, and have a lovely smell. They are a kind of panacea to the Japanese. Kanazawa used to carry them with him, and if you received an injury, he'd give you one. But I don't think that you can put them on damaged skin. We were so honoured to get a Salonpas. It was worth getting bruised just so that you could have one!

"John Chisholm worked as a stage rigger at Elstree Studios, and he met all the film stars. He opened a *dojo* in Chiswick, and invited a few people down. He arranged for Kanazawa and Enoeda to give demonstrations and for sample lessons to be given. I attended these 'celebrity affairs'. On the first occasion, Lee Marvin and John Cassavetes came along. They were making the film *The Dirty Dozen* at the time. They sat and watched the training, and I think they were quite overawed by it to be truthful. I mean they played the hard guys in the films, with the machine-guns, throwing hand grenades and so on, but they weren't really like that. They were actors. In real life they were quiet and subdued. I mean they had the rugged faces of men of action for which they were famous, but they were just ordinary people to be honest. I remember that after the demonstration, Kanazawa broke a brick for them with a punch. The brick was held by Eddie and John Chisholm. There's a photo of that somewhere.

Master Kanazawa breaks a brick held by Eddie Whitcher and John Chisholm, whilst actors Lee Marvin and John Cassavetes look on.

"In February, 1966, Andy Sherry and Joe Chialton were awarded their black-belts from Enoeda *Sensei*. When we heard this news, certain members of the London *dojo* were very surprised. Don't get me wrong though, I'm not for one minute saying that the two new *Dan* grades didn't deserve them or anything like that, I'm sure they did, and I certainly wasn't in a position to judge in any case, but I'm just saying a few eyebrows were raised, and I'll tell you why. Jimmy Neal had started training in 1959, a year or so before the Liverpool boys joined the BKF. Jimmy was an instructor for the BKF, was graded 1st kyu by Murakami, and had taught at the Liverpool *dojo*. He trained really hard, and it was commonly thought, at least by the members of the London *dojo*, that he would be the first to be awarded the black belt, because of his seniority. At the time, we thought he was the highest JKA graded Shotokan student in Britain, with Wingrove now gone. Actually, we were wrong, because I have since learned that Jack Green, of Blackpool, was graded 2nd kyu at the end of June, 1965, when Kanazawa visited Blackpool. When Kanazawa regraded us a few weeks later, Neal was awarded 2nd kyu too. In September of that year, I now learn, Sherry and Chialton graded to 2nd kyu under Kanazawa. So by September, 1965, there were four BKF 2nd kyu in Britain and by November, Eddie Whitcher, John Chisholm and Rob Williams had joined them.

"The next thing we knew was that Sherry, Chialton and Green had been awarded their *shodans*. I recall there being a fairly heated discussion, raised voices in fact, about that between two particular people – but Jimmy Neal wasn't involved. Someone had his ear used as a verbal *makiwara*, you might say. I think that was at Lyndhurst Hall, although I can't be certain. It wasn't a question of it being a race for the distinction of being the first JKA graded black-belt in Great Britain, I don't think, but it was felt that Jimmy had missed out badly. [No 1st kyu at this time are recorded in the BKF grading register, but this does not necessarily mean that 1st kyu gradings did not take place]. Kanazawa *Sensei* awarded Neal a black-belt without a grading, virtually immediately afterwards, a matter of days, if memory serves. However, Jimmy Neal seems to have lost interest after that, and he just stopped coming to the *dojo* one day. There were a lot of rumours going around of course, and I don't actually know why he left, but I fancy he must have felt a little bit disheartened by it all. I know I would have been.

"My next grading, the last under the BKF, was on the 23rd February, 1966, when I passed my 3rd kyu, with sixty points, and wore the coverted brown belt. That was regarded as a big step forward. I received average marks for my basics, but was marked down on both *kata* and *kumite*. The grading fee remained unchanged at ten bob [ten shillings – 50p]. At brown-belt we practised freestyle, proper, for the first time. This was *dojo* freestyle and we didn't have any competitions within the club or any nonsense like that. Kanazawa *Sensei* said that freestyle wasn't important at all, and he'd get two brown-belts up during a break, and let them 'pogo' around the *dojo*. Of course real karate has nothing to do with freestyle at all, in my opinion. I learned that from my teacher, who won the JKA *kumite* title. He could easily have made something of that if he'd wanted to, because he was the tops. A few years later, I was picked for a British team and fought against a Japanese team at Crystal Palace, so I too could make something of it. But it just isn't important. Funakoshi knew it, Kanazawa *Sensei* knew it, and now I know it."

Michael Randall's three grading successes under Kanazawa and the British Karate Federation were recorded in the BKF grading register as numbers 583, 717 and 759, respectively.

Michael Randall continued: "I remember that Eddie Whitcher and Rob Williams graded to 1st kyu the same night I got my 3rd kyu.

I was now the same grade as Ray Fuller, and another chap [Harry Peters] got 2nd kyu. Nick and Chris Adamou gained 5th kyu along with John Goodbody; 'Tiger' Nightingale was awarded temporary 4th kyu, I think; Jack Johnson, Peter Lebasci and Mick Peachey got their 4th kyu. 3rd kyu was an important grade because you learned the *kata Bassai-dai*, and that, like occasionally practising freestyle, was seen as a definite step in the right direction.

"Two months later, Eddie took his black-belt grading under Kanazawa at Lyndhurst Hall, and passed. So, like Sherry and Chialton, he too only had to wait a short period before taking his *Dan* grade. That seems quite strange to me today. He was the first student to take a JKA Shotokan *Dan* grading in Britain under Kanazawa. If memory serves me correctly, Rob Williams followed a few months later, then came Ray, but I'm jumping a bit ahead of myself here.

"There were problems brewing, and towards the end of Kanazawa's one year tenure, as it were, things got a bit heated at times. Vernon Bell would often just walk into the *dojo* when Kanazawa was teaching and wander around. Kanazawa wasn't at all happy about this state of affairs, and fair enough after all. He would just bite his tongue and put up with it. However, the next, and last time Bell tried it, Kanazawa shouted him out. It was the first time that Kanazawa had lost his temper with Bell. At the end, Kanazawa had just had enough. It was the final straw. I think it was a culmination of things to be truthful, and it wasn't just Bell's fault, I'm sure. I believe that the BKF had financial matters to consider, and Bell appeared to be a worried man; the stress was showing. His home life wasn't easy either. Believe me, I knew the sort of thing he was going through.

"Because Kanazawa was not that happy about things, the students 'in the know' weren't generally happy either. A number of the senior grades had fairly nasty altercations with Bell, and he threatened to expel them from the BKF. I believe that Kanazawa didn't particularly want to go back to Japan after his one year contract with the BKF had run out. He liked English students and had made a good life for himself. We tried to keep him in the country, we really did, but we weren't successful. We were just working class lads and we were up against things that we didn't understand, and we didn't have any money for lawyers and that kind of thing. Enoeda stayed in Liverpool, so the Liverpool lads were okay.

"I remember going with some of the other faithful students to see

JAPAN KARATE ASSOCIATION.

(Incorporate by Charter in Japan).

GRADING APPLICATION.

CLUB BRITISH KARATE FEDERATION

SURNAME RANDALL   FIRST NAME(S) ROBERT MICHAEL

ADDRESS 3 SOUTHWELL HS. DATE OF BIRTH 8-4-44

BOLEYN RD. N16.

PREVIOUS KARATE EXPERIENCE 2 YEARS 2 MONTHS

OCCUPATION CARPENTER

EXAMINERS NAME KANAZAWA

PRESENT GRADE	BASIC	FORM	KUMITE	TOTAL	RESULT	EXAMINERS REMARKS
4th KYU	5.5	5.5	5.5	60	3	

EXAMINATION FEE [10/-] ubell.   DATE OF EXAMINATION 23-2-66.

AMOUNT RETURNED [ ]

4th KYU & UNDER   =   10/-.

3rd KYU & ABOVE   =   £1/0/-.   IF EXAMINEE OF 3rd KYU & ABOVE FAILS THE GRADING, THE SUM OF 10/- WILL BE RETURNED.

SHODAN   =   £2. 0. 0.   ON FAILING £1.10.0. RETURNED.

NI-DAN   =   £2.10. 0.   ON FAILING £2. 0.0. RETURNED.

SAN-DAN   =   £3. 0. 0.   ON FAILING £2.10.0. RETURNED.

CERTIFICATES OF PROFICIENCY OF THE J.K.A. ARE AWARDED TO ALL GRADES ABOVE 3rd KYU.

N. G. Registry No. 759 19/3/66 ubell.

49.

Michael's third grading application form, under Kanazawa, when he was awarded 3rd kyu.

Michael's BKF licence showing his grading record to 3rd kyu.

Michael, stretching, as a 3rd kyu.

Kanazawa off at Heathrow Airport, to thank him for all he had given us. That was a very sad day.

"When *Sensei* left, the London *dojo* was completely deflated. We didn't know what to do. We were lost without the master. He was the guiding light. He had taken us along a structured path, but when he went, we didn't know what the next step was. We were left without an instructor – aimless. It wasn't as though there were any 3rd Dans, who would have known what to do. We would at least have had the karate then, but we would have still missed the man. There was no sense of inspiration or effort in the club – no spirit. No one really wanted to teach, and there was a dreadful void in our lives. It was as if he'd been killed, suddenly, and we were in shock, and then mourning. We longed to have him back and took it upon ourselves to do something about the situation. If Bell wasn't going to renew his contract, or couldn't renew it, then we, the students, would!"

IV

A NEW ASSOCIATION

Michael Randall continued: "We tried to get *Sensei* back immediately, but a certain person put a block on it. I don't know why, but I can guess. On two or three occasions we went to the Home Office to deal with the authorities there, and it was they who told us who was blocking the application, and we couldn't get a work permit. They said that they were considering what to do, but this type of bureaucracy can go on forever.

"We all had a meeting at Lyndhurst Hall to discuss what was going to happen now that Kanazawa *Sensei* was no longer in the country. I don't remember whether we asked Bell to organize it or whether Bell called it, but the boys from the Liverpool club came down. It was fairly heated at times as I recall, and certain things were agreed, but Bell said that there weren't enough people in attendence to carry a vote, which I thought was ridiculous, because everybody was there who had to be there.

"When the meeting broke up, the Liverpool lads got in their cars and drove back home, and members of the London *dojo* went down the pub, the Admiral Napier, to have a drink and chat about what was to be done. I believe that it was there and then, or possibly one evening after training, that it was decided to form the Karate Union of Great Britain, but we didn't have a clue how to go about it. We were just lads in our twenties, so we didn't have any knowledge of what the procedure for setting up an association was. Eddie thought of the name. We were a bit worried about two things concerning the Karate Union of Great Britain. Firstly, we thought that it sounded like the Russian Secret Service, the KGB, which was very much in the news in those days. Secondly, we weren't sure about the word "union". We didn't want a working class tag put onto the practice of karate, for people from all walks of life practised the art. You know, "If you want to study karate, you have to join a union." We decided

The Admiral Napier, in Warden Road, Kentish Town, where, it is argued, the notion of forming the KUGB was first formulated.

that "union" could mean other things as well. The bringing together of Shotokan karateka, for example, and we wanted a name that would be useful for encompassing, England, Scotland, Wales and Northern Ireland. The Karate Union of Great Britain also had the advantage of having "karate" as the opening word. We thought that would help on the advertising front. To be truthful however, these were grand plans, but all we wanted to do was practise karate with Kanazawa – nothing else seemed to matter. If it meant a single *dojo* in Great Britain, so be it, we didn't care. I don't quite know how that tied up with the Liverpool members, but I think we went up there, to Manchester actually, to Holdsworth Hall, to formalize things. I know it has been said that the KUGB was formed up north, and perhaps it was officially, I can't remember, but I can tell you that it was decided in London, in the Admiral Napier, to call it the KUGB. But does it really matter in any case? The KUGB has survived more than thirty years and is still very strong, with loyal members. A handful of karateka like Andy Sherry, Terry O'Neill, Bob Poynton, Gordon Thompson, Ian MacLaren and Charles Naylor are original members.

"It wasn't long before the administration went up north though. You see they had the expertise, the know how, and the interest of being in charge of it. A chap called Terry Heaton, who was just a karate kyu grade at the time, had a large office, secretaries, and so on, in Manchester, and he wanted to do all the admin'. We didn't want to know about all that in London, we only wanted to do karate. Time spent attending endless meetings could be far better spent training – that was our way of looking at it then. Heaton became the secretary to the association, and a chap called Terry Astley, from Liverpool, became the treasurer. When the KUGB became established, Mick Peachey and I used to go up north fairly frequently to represent London, and *Sensei* used to come with us sometimes.

"Kanazawa may have gone to France in the meantime, I can't remember, to give us time to get him a work permit and to sort out a new *dojo*. Lyndhurst Hall was Bell's of course, and out of bounds, and we didn't think that the Kentish Town Baths would want us back, so we had to find him somewhere else. Meanwhile, then, Nick and Chris Adamou found the Blackfriars *dojo*, the John Marshall Hall, in Blackfriars Road, just south of the Thames, and not far from Blackfriars Bridge, which was to be *Sensei's* London headquarters. That was a lovely *dojo*, and it had underfloor heating, which was glorious, and such a change from the ice-cold stone floor of the Kentish Town Baths.

"Eventually, Kanazawa was allowed back, but I can't recall now how we managed it. What I do remember, however, is an hilarious story associated with his trouble coming through Customs on landing at Heathrow. We were waiting for *Sensei* at the arrival lounge, and we knew that he was on the flight because in those days they had flight registers that you could consult. The plane arrived, and we

Outside the Blackfriars *dojo*. The grassy area is the old graveyard (see later).

waited and waited. All the passengers disembarked and collected their luggage, but *Sensei* was nowhere to be seen. We seemed to wait hours, and the reason why was that someone had informed the authorities that Kanazawa was a spy. Kanazawa told us that they went through his luggage with a fine tooth comb, and the delay was due to *Sensei's* scarf. This was an odd scarf, because it had a map of a country on it, and I think that the Customs officials thought that it contained some hidden information. On future occasions, we had no problems.

"Actually, later on, we did have a spy in the country, if you are to believe it. This story is even funnier. He was a young Japanese, and his first name was ——. He was supposed to be an industrial spy, but was a cook by profession, and was over here to learn some secrets about preserving techniques, or something daft like that. Mind you, he couldn't have been much of a spy if we all knew about it! His cover was that he was in this country learning English. He took up karate at the Blackfriars *dojo*. *Sensei* quickly became friends with him of course, being Japanese. Anyway, and this will make you laugh, this chap was supposed to be an expert cook, and one evening we all went out for a Chinese meal. We sat around the table and ordered spare ribs, where you have to use your fingers to eat. When we'd all finished, the waiters came around with the finger bowls, so that we

Inside the Blackfriars *dojo*. Pauline Bindra (nee Laville) is show in the process of blocking. Standing by the wooden partition is Miyoko Ohta, Michael's future wife, who went on to attain 3rd kyu. To Pauline's immediate right is William Mannion – 1966/67.

could wash our fingers. Each finger bowl had water in it and a slice of lemon. *Sensei* went, "Ohhhh! and was looking at this —— fellow. —— had picked up his finger bowl and was drinking the water in it. *Sensei* spoke to him in Japanese. It was so embarrassing because — was supposed to be the food expert, and he thought that it was a bowl of soup that had come up!

"When *Sensei* came back from Europe, we secured a nice flat for him down in Richmond. I think John Chisholm found it, and I kitted it out for him with someone else, but I can't remember who. Later, when Kanazawa left Britain for Germany, Enoeda *Sensei* moved south, and lived in it.

"So, when Kanazawa returned, it was to a nice new *dojo* and a newly formed association. He was handed it on a plate, but we just had to have him. Looking back, I must say that I feel very sorry for the way Vernon Bell was treated. It was most regretable, but seemingly unavoidable. He had built Shotokan karate up in this country from nothing, and was left virtually high and dry. If Bell felt bitter, I couldn't blame him; I couldn't blame him at all. At the time though, it must be said that he was intransigent. He tried to assert his authority. He dug his heels in and attempted to save all that he had worked for. He tried to make others buckle under, like he'd done in the past. This had worked for him then, when he was the only black-belt in the country, but not any more. There were other black-belts now.

"I must say that I have nothing but praise for Bell, and the karate association he founded. He's an old man now and largely forgotten, but I haven't forgotten him, and never will. I should like to take this opportunity to thank him for everything he gave me. The BKF standards were high, make no mistake about it. With the arrival of the Japanese he could not realistically compete, no one could. I believe that things might have been different if toleration had been exercised, but, regretably, it was not. We thought Bell a distant man, severe and odd, but I now know that we were wrong. If someone left karate, he didn't seem to care, but now I realise that he cared a great deal. It was an act. He remembers virtually every student of the early BKF and could tell you a little story about each of them. That's more than I could ever do. He had a heart. He had deep feelings, but he never showed them. Perhaps that's where he went wrong?"

V

ONE OF THE SEVEN SAMURAI

Michael Randall continued: "When I was a brown-belt, during the breaks in the lessons, Kanazawa would call me out to practise Sumo with him. I think Kanazawa *Sensei* respected Sumo. Everyone else would sit cross-legged at the edge of the *dojo* and have a rest, and he'd call me up. "Now you must try very hard," he'd say. We'd grab hold of each other's belts and we'd lean into one another and then off we'd go. Well actually, it was off I'd go. *Sensei* would just lower his centre of gravity and spread the weight on his feet in a *shiko-dachi* type stance. I'd push and try to lift for all I was worth for about fifteen to twenty seconds. Then that was that. I was worn out. You can't sustain maximum effort like that for very long, and remember, I was doing this after a tiring full day's work and an exhausting karate lesson, when everyone else was resting! I'd try for about thirty seconds in all I suppose, and just fade badly at the end, then bow, and sit down. The whole purpose of the exercise was for me to build up power from resistance of course, and to generate power from low down. That was excellent training, and somehow it worked. After finishing a bout of Sumo with *Sensei*, I felt more enlivened. I found it very difficult to come out of myself. I was held back, withdrawn, and that Sumo really helped me. It was as though I'd restrain my spirit in karate training, but after the Sumo I found that I could let all my spirit out, in a *kiai*, for example. I was so shy, but I learned to *kiai* with full vigour and I shall always be grateful to *Sensei* for sorting that out. I did manage to surprise him on one occasion, when I actually pushed him back – just a little bit. He didn't know I could do that, and, to tell you the truth, nor did I!

"Another thing that Kanazawa did to help me build myself up was to teach me the kata *Hangetsu* before taking my black-belt. He taught it to me alone, no one else, privately. I weighed only nine and a half stone, and I needed more weight, more muscle, and he told me

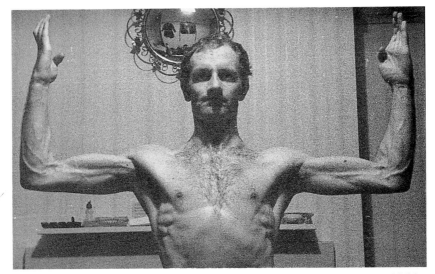

The physique Michael gained, partly from his training in *Hangetsu* - 1966.

that the practice of *Hangetsu* would help me. I think that *Hangetsu* was *Sensei's* favourite *kata* at that time. Continued practice of that *kata* seemed to have worked, and I built up a fine set of abdominal muscles. Muscle is dense, so it is heavier than fat. Fat's no good for karate at all, and begs all sorts of questions about the owner. *Hangetsu* is a marvellous *kata* for improving one's focus as well, of course. I suppose, because I was the only one in the London *dojo* to have been shown that *kata*, it became a favourite of mine. It made me feel a bit special, and I actually chose *Hangetsu* for my *Nidan* grading.

"The hard and repetitive nature of Kanazawa's lessons provided a good grounding not only for one's technique, but also life in general. He would ask us to perform say, twenty *gyaku-zuki*, with maximum effort, and then move onto another technique, and that would be performed with maximum effort as well. He would say that Sumo wrestlers are so good because they train one hundred percent for a short period in the day, perhaps only half an hour, and rest and eat the remainder of the time. It is the explosive nature of Sumo that the wrestlers seek and not stamina, as such. Stamina is not really required. Karate, *Sensei* said, was like Sumo. One doesn't have a ten minute match, it's all over in a few seconds, and that's what he trained us for.

"However, having said that, occasionally, very occasionally, he

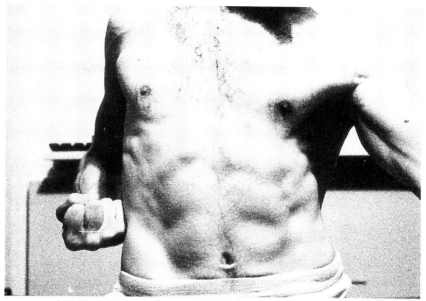

Michael displays his powerful abdominal muscles – 1966.

would train us into the ground. I remember a number of such lessons, spread out over the years. One particular session was at the Kentish Town Baths one Friday evening, when we were still with the BKF. During the five minute break, Mick Peachey and I literally staggered out of the *dojo*, to go to the changing room to swill some water around our mouths. We never drank the cold water though, mainly because you'd get stomach cramps. We both sat down on the bench and when the time came to get back up, our legs wouldn't support us – we'd practised that many kicks and deep stances. Our legs were really like jelly. That lesson was the most intensive karate session I've ever been in. You don't get lessons like that today. I think the reason Kanazawa gave us those odd lessons was to say, "If you can get through that, you can get through anything!"

"Whereas Kanazawa's philosophy seemed to be twenty techniques with maximum effort, in each technique, when it was fast to count, as I've explained, other Japanese instructors of the time didn't necessarily instruct in the same manner. One, for example, used to get the students to perform say, one hundred *gyaku-zuki*, but it is impossible to put maximum effort into so many punches, so I liked Kanazawa's way of thinking. Mind you, practising one hundred techniques at a time, does, I suppose, clear the neural pathways so

Michael as a 1st kyu – 1966.

that the action of a punch becomes second nature. It's roundabouts and swings, I suppose.

"I can't remember exactly when the KUGB was formed, but it must have been around the middle of 1966. Not long afterwards I took my 2nd kyu, and a few months after that, my 1st kyu, both under Kanazawa. I don't have the dates for these gradings anymore, but they were definitely in 1966, for I took my *shodan* grading on the 6th January, 1967, at the Blackfriars *dojo*.

"I can't say that I did any special preparation for my *shodan*, I simply trained very hard under Kanazawa and Takahashi [see shortly]. In those days, getting a black-belt was viewed slightly differently, I think. It was seen as a product of hard training, and not so much as a special step. Nowadays, it tends to be more structured. I believe that there are technically good and technically bad *shodans* today, but in those days you had to be good to pass, otherwise you kept failing. They wouldn't pass you if there was any fault in your technique. Nowadays, I think a lot is to do with character, age, and ability, and if a student hasn't necessarily got good technique, but trains extremely hard, he is passed on merit, or other qualities. In the past, that wouldn't have happened. In those days, we were all very fit lads in our twenties. The training was physically very hard, as I've said, and if you couldn't keep up, you fell by the wayside. Today, we try to cater for all and sundry, and if someone is keen and dedicated but of questionable technique, they can still pass. In some ways it's better these days, but I have to say that I think the standard for black-belt is generally lower.

"Nowadays, we have the oral/interview as part of the black-belt grading, and the student is required to be quite knowledgeable on karate before they pass. We didn't have anything like that when I graded. We only had a fragmentary knowledge of the history of Shotokan, for example. There were no books around really.

"My *shodan* was a kind of private grading, because no one else was attempting a black-belt and no one was allowed to watch the Dan grading. Mind you, there must have been other people there, because I had to do freestyle against three separate people. The basics were gruelling. My *tokui* [favourite or chosen] *kata* was *Enpi*. I always liked *Enpi*. I think *Sensei* influenced me in my choice. He said that *Enpi* meant "flying swallow" and it was about graceful movements. It suited someone like me, with a lighter build. We practised the *kata* with a *mawashi-geri* instead of the *fumikomi* even in those days. I still practise the *kata* that way, but I understand that Kanazawa has

Michael, as a 1st Dan, performing *age-uke* – 1967.

reverted to the stamping-kick. We knew even then that Kanazawa taught it differently, because we saw the Liverpool lads performing the *kata* the way they had been taught by Enoeda *Sensei*, and they practised it with the *fumikomi*. Other Japanese performed it with the stamping-kick as well.

"As part of my grading, Kanazawa asked me to show a few practical interpretations from *Enpi*. I could choose whatever I wanted. I remember that I chose *tekubi-kake-uke* as one of the techniques, but I can't recall the others now after all these years.

"Kanazawa also asked me to punch at a pencil, which he held. He called me up to the table, behind which he was sitting, dressed in shirt, tie and jacket – Kanazawa always looked smart – and moved the pencil up and down, side to side, backwards and forwards. Each time he stopped, I was to punch at it, but not actually hit it. The punch was to stop a few centimetres away, with full focus. I believe

Michael, as a 1st Dan, performing *gyaku-zuki* – 1967.

the reason for that little exercise was to test distancing, reaction-time and focus.

"Talking of differences in *kata*, I also remember that Kanazawa taught me to *kiai* on the crescent-kick at the end of *Hangetsu*, which I believe he still does, though many other teachers perform the second *kiai* on the *gedan-zuki* following the kick.

"In those days, you weren't informed of your grading result there and then, although you were under the BKF. That went for any grading, under Kanazawa, once the KUGB was formed. Kanazawa wouldn't always let you know at the next lesson either. I think part of the Japanese way was that you had to wait, to learn patience. After all, it's only a grading and a bad result is not going to stop you training, is it? If it is, then there is something wrong. I think he kept me waiting perhaps a couple of months – or at least it seemed liked

115

Michael, as a 1st Dan, performing *teisho-kosa-uke* from the *kata Enpi* - 1967.

that! – before he told me I'd passed my *shodan*. I like the method; it's good. It's a test of character and a test of staying power – things like that. One evening, at Blackfriars, we passed in the corridor, and Kanazawa said to me, "Oh! Mr. Randly. Your black-belt is in my car." That was a lovely moment and I shall never forget it. He gave me the keys to his car, which was parked in Colombo Street, opposite the Rose and Crown pub, and the belt was in the glove compartment.

The Rose and Crown in Colombo Street was frequented by members of the Blackfriars *dojo*. It was outside this pub that Michael collected his black belt from Master Kanazawa's car's glove compartment.

Michael's KUGB Dan grade card signed by Chief Instructor, Hirokazu Kanazawa, and National Secretary, Terry Heaton.

That was the first night I wore it. Kanazawa always bought the silk black belt for you, and that made it seem extra special. It was his way of saying well done.

"I wore that belt until it went almost white, and when I got another belt, so as not to lose the spirit of my first black belt, I asked my mother to cut out a small section, about six inches, and insert it into my next belt. That's gone as well, and I wish I'd kept that too.

"After gaining my black-belt, the first *kata* Kanazawa *Sensei* taught me was *Tekki Nidan*. A few months after that, I started a *dojo* up at the Alms House, Balls Pond Road, in Hackney. That was my first *dojo*, and I had a few students. The club then moved to St. Michael's Church Hall, which was in, or near Hackney, and then we moved again to a judo *dojo* above a Jewish Boys' Club in Amhurst Road, Stoke Newington. Then the club moved to Woodford."

Nick Adamou recalled a little aside at this time: "Mick had just received his *shodan* under Kanazawa *Sensei*, and I remember talking about some of the many, many things that we thought would be difficult, if not impossible, to attain in karate. Mick explained to me that he wished he could have the incredible spirit that Kanazawa *Sensei* showed when he practised freestyle, and he wished he could 'turn it on' too, just like that, in an instant. Mick had noticed that Kanazawa *Sensei* could be calm, happy and relaxed one moment, and an instant later have great fighting spirit."

Michael's freestyle was pretty good though, to say the least, prior

Michael Performs *yoko-geri-kekomi* – 1967/68.

Michael performs a superb *yoko-geri-kekomi* - 1968.

to his taking his black-belt, as another story by Nick Adamou shows: "Mick was a brown-belt at the time and we were all training under Kanazawa *Sensei* at the Blackfriars *dojo*. The master decided to let pairs come up, to practise freestyle in front of the class. Mick's partner on this occasion was Stan Longstaff, who was also a brown-belt, I believe. Stan's facial expression, along with his body language, was that of quiet acceptance of the fact that he was just not good at this [compared to Michael Randall], and was never, ever, going to be – that's the inevitability of things, and that's the way it is. Stan had a happy smile of acceptance and a way of pushing his lips together each time a situation came along to prove him right in his negative outlook.

"Both Mick and Stan bowed to one another and Stan got underway with a *chudan oi-zuki*, and at the same time Mick delivered a *jodan mawashi-geri*. It was all over in seconds and Stan was smiling with that, "Didn't I tell you all it was inevitable?" look, and, "I'm sorry I bothered you all." Mick looked as if he didn't own the kick, as it went in so quickly.

"Mick and Stan were asked to have another go, and again, as Stan attacked with a *chudan mae-geri*, I believe, Mick moved gracefully to Stan's right and performed a right *jodan haito-uchi*."

Stanley Longstaff at the time, 1966, was an unmarried, thirty-seven year old pipe welder from South London, who worked for G.N. Haden and Sons Ltd, in the Euston Road. He had served in the Royal Navy for twelve years and had interests in philosophy, psychic and occult studies. His application for BKF membership was dated the 16th September, 1964, and he had studied judo previously. The poor chap seems to have been plagued by Michael Randall, and Nick Adamou as well. Nick recalled another incident, before the start of a lesson at the London *dojo*: "I walked across the large hall which we used on Friday evenings and said "*Oss*" to Stan, who was limbering up on the floor beside the stage. As an eighteen year old, I was very supple, and I always wanted to get even more supple. I therefore would always tell myself, and others, how stiff I was, in order to push myself and never to get complacent. Mick Randall also arrived, and we said "*Oss*", and got on with our various limbering up exercises. Both Mick and I began practising *mawashi-geri* over the stage. Mick's slow *mawashi-geri* was about six inches higher than mine, and I quietly muttered to myself how stiff I was. It seemed to me that Stan broke when he heard my words and, looking at Mick's leg, which was four inches above his own head, and looking at mine, which

Michael performs a fine *yoko-tobi-geri* - 1968.

was at my head height, said, "Oh yes Nick. Of course you are *so* stiff. I mean just look at your leg. It is only head height and look at Mick's, it's only four inches above his head!" I hasten to add that all of this was said in the best of humour and good heartedness."

Michael Randall recalled two other stories about his freestyle during this period and a further one on suppleness. Michael continued: "I remember that Charles Mack came down to the Blackfriars *dojo* one evening and brought a team with him. Mack had trained in Japan to *nidan* in Shotokan under Nakayama, but was most notable as a judoka. He was the first man from Great Britain to be awarded a 5th Dan from the Kodokan. Anyway, Mack had one or two *dojo* in London, and we had an inter-club competition. I actually won the freestyle, but I don't remember the incident for that, but rather for receiving a punch on my forehead. I saw stars alright, it really rocked my brain. I sat down in the *dojo* after I'd won, with my back facing the chapel, with my head in my hands. The punch brought on a nasty migraine, and I felt really sick.

"The first KUGB National Championships were held in the summer of 1967 [22nd July] at Alexandra Palace, and I entered the *kumite* and team *kumite* events. It was a big occasion and everyone was full of expectation. Masters Kanazawa, Enoeda and Shirai were all there. I don't think I entered the *kata*, but I can't recall why. Anyway, I reached the last eight in the *kumite*. I remember that Jack Green won the *kumite* title with a *jodan uraken* upon Andy Sherry. The London *kumite* team was made up of Eddie Whitcher, Rob Williams, Ray Fuller, Sam Firlej and myself, as I recall. We faced Liverpool Red Triangle in the final. We won, or drew, the first two bouts, and I was up against Andy Sherry and drew with him. Bob Poynton clinched it for Liverpool on the last bout if I remember correctly, but it was a very close thing. I was personally really pleased with my result, because we never really practised freestyle. There were only three events contested that evening, and the *kata* went to Andy Sherry, who performed a nice *Enpi*.

"I lost interest in competition after that. Well, that's not actually true, for I was never interested in karate competition – full-stop. I went in for the first KUGB championships because Kanazawa picked me to enter, and I couldn't really refuse. I have never thought that karate was about competing. Karate is a martial art and competitions down-grade it in my view.

"I remember that Nick Adamou reached the final of the *kata* competition in 1968, but had to withdraw due to injury, which was a shame. Blackfriars reached the semi-finals in the team *kumite* event that year and Ray Fuller made it to the last eight in the individual event. Master Nakayama came over from Japan especially to see the championships. He performed a *kata* to music. Masters Miyazaki and Asano were at the championships as well, and were both ranked 4th Dan. The Japanese performed a number of demonstrations, including wood-breaking, and defences against knife and chair

Masters Kanazawa and Shirai give a demonstration of *ippon-kumite* at the KUGB's first National Championships – Alexandra Palace, 1967.

KUGB's 1967 championships. Michael Randall can be seen standing in the audience behind Shirai's back leg, and in line with his back foot.

attacks. I remember that Ray received a special certificate and a silver tie pin from Nakayama *Sensei*, for his work in Shotokan. In 1969, Chris Adamou was the runner-up in the *kata* event, which was excellent. He performed *Enpi*, as did the winner, Andy Sherry. Once again, Blackfriars reached the semi-finals."

On the subject of stretching, brought up by Nick Adamou earlier, Michael Randall had an interesting story concerning Satoshi Miyazaki: "I remember Miyazaki well," Michael recalled. "He was a very nice man – warm and friendly. His form was brilliant of course, that goes without saying, but he was incredibly supple as well. I can't recall which *dojo* the story I'm about to tell you happened in, though it was almost certainly either Blackfriars or Garth Hall [see below]. Anyway, there were two sets of wheels in the corner of the *dojo*, like large skateboards. I haven't a clue what they were used for, nor why they were in the *dojo*. I remember that Miyazaki went up to them, inspected these curious objects, and carefully stood astride them, one under each foot. He then slowly let the 'skateboards' slide away from him, one in one direction and the other in the opposite direction, until he was in a full side splits. What was particularly amazing about this feat was that he went well beyond the horizontal, in that the base of his torso was below the height of his legs and feet. His toes were pointing in the direction that he was looking in – straight forward. I thought that I was pretty supple, I worked hard at it, but what Miyazaki did was phenomenal. It is therefore not surprising that I remember him for his kicks. He had a devastating *kekomi* that shot out like lightning and locked as if there was no tomorrow.

"I also recall that Miyazaki had an off-set eye, and that he smoked. He went to live and teach for the JKA in Belgium. I read a few years ago that he had died of cancer [in 1993]. He was a great man, and his death was an important loss to Shotokan.

"I remember something else about wheels! At the Blackfriars *dojo* there was a very large grand piano that was in the corner of the church hall. One day, Kanazawa *Sensei* thought that it was in the way, so he walked over to it and tried to lift it up! He was going to put it out of the way, on the stage. He tried to lift this enormous piano as if it were made of cardboard! He bent down and put his hands underneath it, but of course it didn't budge. No one can lift a piano! He was totally amazed that he couldn't lift it. He really believed he could do it, but I don't think he knew what a piano was. He just thought that it was a piece of furniture that lifted. We all just laughed and said, "*Sensei*! It doesn't lift!" I think he beckoned over a few of

Master Miyazaki loosening up.

Satoshi Miyazaki performs a *chudan mae-kekomi* on his opponent.

Master Enoeda giving a display at an early KUGB championship.

Masters Kanazawa and Asano giving a display of self-defence.

Masters Kanazawa and Enoeda sparring on Hampstead Heath – 1967.

After blocking Mick Peachey's *mae-geri* Kanazawa blocks and counters to Master Enoeda – 1967.

Masters Kanazawa and Enoeda sparring on Hampstead Heath – 1967.

Master Kanazawa demonstrating *kata* application from *Heian Yondan* – 1967.

us to help him, but of course we couldn't budge it either. It just stayed there, that's where it lived, and we jolly well had to train with it there. We often spoke about that very curious incident.

"My first experience of teaching karate, under Kanazawa *Sensei's* guidance, was at Blackfriars. We trained with the chapel side of the *dojo* to our backs, and the stage, which is no longer there, to our right. One evening a very tall, powerfully built man, named Alan Clemens, and his brother-in-law, whose Christian name was Richard, came along to watch, and Kanazawa asked me to teach them *gedan-*

Master Enoeda demonstrating *kata* application from *Hangetsu* – 1967.

barai and *zenkutsu-dachi* upon the stage, whilst he taught the rest of the class in the *dojo* proper, as it were. I was a brown-belt at the time – 3rd kyu I think.

"There were three main KUGB London clubs at the time, as I recall. The Blackfriars *dojo*, Chisholm's Chiswick Club, and another, which opened up a few months later, at Garth Hall, in Golders Green. Garth Hall was a community hall about a mile away from Golders Green station, and we used to walk it. The *dojo* had a nice, composite floor, and bright lighting. The club was founded by a certain Dr. Ralph Blair-Gould, who was just a low kyu grade at the time. He was much older than us, his hair was greying, and he wore a beard and glasses. I don't think that he was a general practitioner, but more of a consultant. He used to have a phrase, "Karate is for the elite." I will always remember the way he said that, in his well-bred accent.

"An incident that I recall at Garth Hall happened when Kanazawa was away. Chisholm brought down some Japanese to the *dojo* who were working on the Bond film, *You Only Live Twice*, which was set partly in Japan. I think Ray was taking the lesson, and they walked in towards the end, to watch. When the session finished, they were introduced, and one of the Japanese performed a *kata* for us. I think the students performed a *kata* for him in return – *Heian Godan*, I believe it was. Another member of the team was a 7th Dan in Iaido – a real master. I remember him showing us his sword and saying that it had a live spirit – that it was alive!

"Talking about film, or being on film, at least in the form of photographs, the magazine, *Karate and Oriental Arts*, was founded around this time. Mick Peachey and I were featured in Number 4. The following year, I think it was, when Kanazawa did his *kata* book on *Kanku-dai*, I would go with *Sensei*, Mick Peachey, and the Adamou brothers, up to Wardour Street in Soho, to have pictures taken. Kanazawa selected me to be the subject of *Heian Nidan*. I had many photographs taken and was asked to do the art work. Kanazawa kept asking me for the art work, but it never appeared, because I didn't know what to do. It may sound daft, but I just didn't know what I was expected to do, and I felt terribly embarrassed about admitting it in those days.

"Kanazawa taught at Garth Hall. As I recall, we trained there once a week, at the Chiswick *dojo* once a week, and at Blackfriars twice a week. I think we also trained at the Plaistow *dojo* around this time, because that would have made my five evenings a week, but I can't for the life of me recall whose *dojo* it was. I do remember that Eddie Whitcher used to take me down to the *dojo* on the back of his motorbike. That thing went like the wind. The acceleration of a Triumph Bonneville is tremendous. I used to hang on for dear life – literally!

"I recall that it was outside the Plaistow *dojo*, which was a school hall, that I saw Kanazawa perform an amazing feat. He was answering a question put by a student after the lesson, and was describing how to make a proper foot for *kekomi*. He was wearing proper black leather shoes with thick soles and heels, and he formed the foot perfectly in the shoe. There was a kind of metamorphosis as the leather moulded and the sole creaked and twisted around the foot. It was incredible. Think of the power of the foot muscles required to be able to do that?

"A number of other Japanese instructors visited the country at this time. Takahashi, a 3rd Dan, became Kanazawa's assistant, and taught mainly at Blackfriars, as I've mentioned. He was always

Katsutaro Takahashi

smiling and happy – a really friendly person, reassuring and kind. He was of medium build and as fast as lightning. People confuse this Takahashi, whose first name was Katsutaro, with the three-time JKA *kata* champion of the early seventies, who was killed in a road accident. His first name was Yoshimasa.

"I remember Takahashi at the Blackfriars *dojo* during a break between lessons eating a bag of cold sausages. They were cooked of course, and he offered them around. He also used to hold a rolled up newspaper which we had to kick in the lesson. I remember him doing that, walking down the line. Later, when Kanazawa went to Germany, in 1968, Takahashi became Enoeda's assistant. Later still, Takahashi went back to Japan to carry on the family business, I think.

Master Nagai instructing at Crystal Palace – 1967-68.

"Akio Nagai was also a 3rd Dan, but senior to Takahashi, though there was not much in it. He was a nice man too, though shorter, stockier than Takahashi, and very powerful. He was also very fast, like all the Japanese. He smoked. He went to Germany, but when in England, he and Takahashi were always together, and good friends. Kanazawa, being senior, was always more aloof.

"I remember Takahashi and Nagai taking it in turns at kicking a vaulting horse with various kicks, though *kekomi* comes most vividly to mind. They were both very good – very sharp. However, even at my stage, I could easily detect a difference in ability between the 3rd Dans and Kanazawa, who by this time was promoted to 6th Dan by the JKA. Takahashi and Nagai were like magicians, but Kanazawa was like a god.

"Kanazawa held Nakayama *Sensei* in very high regard, and talking about kicks, I remember that Kanazawa said that Nakayama could perform the legendary triangular jump-kick, which he called *kaku-tobi-geri*. I'm not sure really what this is to be truthful, but Kanazawa was full of admiration for the fact that Nakayama could do it. There is something supposedly mystical about the technique.

"The summer of 1967 was hot, and although the Blackfriars *dojo* was quite cool, sited in a large Victorian building, next to a cold stone chapel, and in the shade of tall plane trees, in the hot months we'd often train outside on the lawn though it was a bit too public for my liking. We did this a number of times under Takahashi, and on one occasion, the last, after training, in the changing rooms, someone joked about the bodies in the graves underneath. Takahashi

Yoshikazu Sumi

caught the conversation and said, "What! You must not joke like that!" The student replied that the lawn *was* a graveyard. Takahashi hurriedly took a coarse brush and scrubbed his feet frantically, trying to get the grass stains off. He was seriously terrified; really frightened. I suppose he thought that it showed a terrific lack of respect training over the bodies of the dead, which of course it does, though the bodies had been removed at the turn of the century. To train on top of a grave would be seen by a Japanese as a disgraceful act. Perhaps he thought that the spirits would come and hound him, punish him, I don't know, but believe me, he was scared.

"Yoshikazu Sumi was another instructor who visited. He was a 3rd Dan too, but he appeared to be an outsider. Takahashi and Nagai would walk away together, laughing, and leave Sumi. I don't think they liked him. It was suggested later that he wouldn't kowtow to

135

Sensei, but I don't know whether that's true. He was a very unusual Japanese, and worthy of studying for his spirit. I remember that on one occasion, during a demonstration at Alexandra Palace, or it may have been Crystal Palace, Kanazawa was heavy handed with Sumi during a freestyle demonstration. He hit him hard across the face, very hard in fact, with the palm of his hand – slapped him, if you like. You could clearly hear the sound of the slap in the audience. It was really quite embarrassing. I took it to be a deliberate "put you in your place" act.

"The other Japanese instructors appeared to largely ignore Sumi, left him on his own. He was a strange guy though. I remember once when he came to the Blackfriars *dojo* with little, round, dark glasses on, and as he went to push open the door, somebody, I forget who he was, kicked the door shut in Sumi's face, without knowing he was there. Sumi ... [reacted] and he frightened the student. I never had a problem with him, never had a run in with him, and was fortunate, but some people did. We were all wary of him though. He was only small, but he was formidable, like all the Japanese instructors. I remember once when he ran over a mountain commando course on Dartmoor in bare feet! That's the sort of man he was, so you had to treat him carefully.

"Sumi used to do *dojo* freestyle with students before the lesson, and he'd catch a few people. But what struck me about him was that he always seemed to be on his own. I remember that once when we went to Heathrow to meet *Sensei* off the plane, Takahashi and Nagai were having fun, and they wouldn't speak to him. It was weird. Sumi was an interesting man though, because he refused to kowtow, or at least that is how it seemed. He later taught karate in Austria.

"Chisholm was still inviting famous actors, and actresses come to that, down to his Chiswick *dojo*, which was the hall in a primary school in Edensor Road. He arranged another demonstration for Peter Sellers, who was interested in karate, and, for a short time, became the first president of the KUGB. Kanazawa and Enoeda gave their usual demonstration. Enoeda performed the *kata Jitte* and Kanazawa performed *Gojushiho-dai*. It was the only time I ever saw Kanazawa perform that form. The power with which Enoeda *Sensei* would perform the three stamping-kicks in *Jitte* was awesome. You could feel the floor vibrate under your feet when he brought his foot down – really!

"Sellers asked if the two Japanese would break some wood for him and they said they would be happy to, and broke some more

Master Kanazawa performs *keito-uke* from the *kata Gojushiho-Dai* (JKA classified).

Master Kanazawa's special Seven Samurai blazer badge, which Michael wore with great pride.

obeche. I think some photographs were taken, humorous ones, with Kanazawa and Enoeda attacking Sellers at the same time, and Sellers defending himself, but for all that, Sellers seemed genuinely interested in karate. The thing I remember about Sellers was that he struck me as a very serious person, and he didn't laugh and crack jokes at all. He looked like someone who worked in an office to be honest, and unless you knew he was a famous actor, you'd never have thought that he was anyone special.

"There were a group of us who followed *Sensei* around, and who trained all the time with him. This little select band, Kanazawa named "The Seven Samurai", and we had a special badge made, which *Sensei* said we should wear on our karate blazer. The Seven Samurai were, Kanazawa, Eddie Whitcher, myself, Nick and Chris Adamou, Mick

Michael and Chris Adamou demonstrate *jiyu-ippon-kumite* – 1968.

Peachey and Will Mannion. We used to frequently go out for meals with Kanazawa and any other visiting Japanese. One of *Sensei's* favourite treats was to go out and have a Chinese meal, because there weren't any Japanese restaurants around in those days, or if there were, we didn't know about them, and I suppose the nearest thing to a Japanese meal was a Chinese meal. We used to go up to China Town, and one restaurant we used to visit was called Sun Luk in Macclesfield Street. Another restaurant we went to was in Piccadilly. Anyway, we got quite friendly with the owners of the Sun Luk, and when we used to go there they let us use the room above the main restaurant. There was a lovely round table up there, and we all used to sit around it.

"Kanazawa had two favourite dishes. The first was sea bass, cooked in ginger and spring onion, and various other things. A whole sea bass would be served up, steaming, on a large oval plate, solely for him. The second meal that *Sensei* favoured was a soup that was served up in a large bowl. I can't remember the name of it, but the soup is full of fish and noodles. Kanazawa used to say, "If you want a body like mine, you must eat fish." Kanazawa's body, of course, was lean and very muscular.

"The Japanese have difficulty pronouncing the letter "F". They can't say "fish", they say "fwish". Anyway, on one occasion – I won't name names, but it wasn't one of the Seven Samurai – we were with Kanazawa *Sensei* and another Japanese. We were all sitting around this table, and Kanazawa was saying, "I like fwish. I like fwish." One of the party, a fellow student, laughing, repeated, "Fwish, fwish, fwish," thinking that Kanazawa's pronunciation was funny. Well, the next minute, the other Japanese in the party nearly took this student's head off. He really slapped him across the face – nearly knocked him off his chair. "Don't make joke about Kanazawa *Sensei*!" the other Japanese instructor said. There was a deadly silence, and we put our heads down and hid our faces in the bowls. The student was just shocked – in a total state of shock. You could see the red hand mark come up across his cheek. The Japanese who cloutted him just carried on eating as if nothing had happened, as did Kanazawa.

"Eddie didn't often come out to meals, and he wasn't at this one. Although he was one of the Seven Samurai, he rarely socialised. His karate, of course, was brilliant, but he never seemed to travel much.

"The worst thing that ever happened to me on the food side, however, was when a group of us went back to a student's house with some food we'd bought from a Take-away. Kanazawa had fish, as usual, and there was one other portion of fish and the rest was chicken. I was the highest grade in the party after *Sensei*, and I had the fish along with Kanazawa. Hierarchy even involved what you

Chris Adamou blocks Michael's *mae-geri* and counters with a masterful *jodan mawashi-geri* – 1968.

ate in those days! Well, the fish was whole, and Kanazawa casually ate the brains and the eyes along with all the connecting tissue. I just watched and then he said to me, "Randly! You must eat the eyes too!" Well, there was no way out of it. That instantly taught me about privilege! I remember the other lads, those with strong stomachs, just watched me as I skewered this dead trout's eye with chopsticks, gouged it out of its socket, quickly put in my mouth – I reasoned that this was my best bet – and swallowed. How I ever did that I just don't know. It makes me sick now just thinking about it. When I swallowed, I almost retched, but at least I thought that that was that, and I'd keep quiet for the rest of the evening and not be so

Chris Adamou counters *chudan mawashi-geri* to Michael's *oi-zuki* –
Walthamstow, 1968.

smug about having the same food as *Sensei*. But when he instructed
me to turn the fish over and eat the other eye, which I did. I must
have gone as white as a ghost. It may sound ridiculous today, but
that's how it was then. He may have been testing me, or teaching me
a lesson, I don't know, but I shall remember the thought of those
cold, lifeless eyes staring at me to my dying day.

"Mind you, Kanazawa told us that he'd eaten some strange things
in his life, and I recall that, for his 5th Dan, he told us that he was
required to eat a mouse and fight a bear. I don't think for one minute
that this was true, but he used the story as a kind of metaphor, a bit
like the tortoise and the hare, or Swift's *Gulliver's Travels*. At the
time though, we believed it, or I certainly did. Now, I think that the
story means that at 5th Dan you must have the resolve to conquer

all, and survive. To be fearless in the pursuit of what you believe to be right. It's a bit like the meaning of *Bassai-dai*, which is often translated as, "to storm a fortress." The moves of that *kata* don't in some way mimic the actions required to take a castle; rather, correct and repetitive practice of the *kata* teaches you to have the strength and resolve to take a fortress, single-handedly if need be, or in other words, overcome all enemies. One of your enemies is fear of the unknown, so perhaps that was why Kanazawa made me eat those eyes? I suppose that overcoming other "enemies" might be interpreted as overcoming life's many disappointments. The "fortress" may be interpreted as everyday life itself. If you loose a loved one, are made redundant and face money worries, or even ruin, the practice of *Bassai-dai* will, I believe, help you through it. Not only that, the regular practice of karate gives you something to hold onto, something that is constant, in an up and down, chaotic world.

"The student who got that heavy clip around the ear used to be a strange chap. I remember once, when we were waiting for a train on the platform. I think we were going to Portsmouth. It was a lovely summer's day and we were just sitting down on the benches, chatting, soaking up the sun, when *Sensei* got up, took a few steps along the platform, and went into *hangetsu-dachi*. This student got up and walked over to *Sensei*, which none of us would ever have done, you know, disturb his quiet state of mind whilst he was pondering on some point, and said, "*Sensei! Sensei!* That stance is so weak! It's weak! It's weak!" The lads watching just tried to bury their heads. *Sensei* just made a groaning sound like, "Errrrrrrr!"

"I remember this same student went up to Kanazawa on another occasion. I don't know what he said to *Sensei*, but Kanazawa turned to me and, pointing his finger to the side of his own head, said, "Stupid! Stupid!"

"I remember that occasionally, very occasionally, *Sensei* would have a meal at a student's house. One such meal was at Mick Peachey's, who lived with his grandmother, I think. Anyway, Mick and myself, Kanazawa and Mick's grandmother, were all sitting around the table one Sunday lunch-time, and *Sensei* asked if he could have the recipe for the soup, because he liked it very much and wanted to make it himself. We all looked at one another, for we hadn't had any soup. Then *Sensei* pointed to the gravy jug. The mistake was a simple one to make, but it is one of those little things I remember about the great man.

"I have another funny story too, about Kanazawa's driving test. I

Nick Adamou performing *tameshiwari*.

think that it involved myself, Chris Adamou and Alan Clemens –
I'll talk about Alan, shortly. *Sensei* wanted to pass his driving test.
He had a Japanese driving licence already, but he had to take a test
again if he wanted to drive in Britain. Well, we took Kanazawa up to
a test centre somewhere fairly near Trafalgar Square, and we all got
in the car with the examiner. The examiner was a small man, round
face, balding, and wearing spectacles. *Sensei* just pulled away, and
we said to the examiner that he should treat this gentleman carefully
because he was a world champion karate instructor. The driving
instructor said we'd better turn back, and the test had finished! But
it was obvious that Kanazawa knew how to drive. That incident was
really funny, and what made it doubly humorous was because another
Japanese we knew couldn't pass his test. This other Japanese used
to drive his car like a tank. He used to drive his face at you. He used
to come out of the *dojo*, get in his car, and drive. He seemed hardly
ever to use the steering wheel. I remember on one occasion we were
crossing the road in front of him, and he nearly ran us down!

"I'll tell you something else that will make you laugh involving
Kanazawa and a car. When Miyoko [Michael's second wife {née
Ohta}, who is Japanese] and I got married, Kanazawa *Sensei* acted
as my best man. At the end of the wedding service all the photographs
were taken, and we were showered with confetti as we walked down
the path to get into the car, so that my new wife and I could be driven

to the reception, which was held at a nice hotel. My father had hired a white Rolls-Royce to take Miyoko and I, and when Kanazawa saw this famous marque glinting in the sunlight, he said, "Ohhhhh! Rolls-Royce! Very, very nice!" and got in it. There we were, the three of us! As the chauffeur drove away, Kanazawa was waving, sedately, out of the window, to all the guests. Miyoko and I didn't have the heart to tell him that the car was intended just for the two of us, because *Sensei* didn't know the protocol and he was so happy to be travelling in a Rolls-Royce."

"I attended quite a few karate courses from 1966 to 1968, and one that I particularly remember was held up on the north-east coast under Kanazawa and Enoeda, but I cannot for the life of me recall where it was. All the northern lads were there – Andy Sherry, Terry O'Neill, Bob Poynton, and so on. We slept in dormitories. I remember it for two particular points. Firstly, we only stayed for about two days because Jack Johnson broke his foot in training, and he wanted to come home, and as he had driven there and was taking us back, we had to go with him. Nick and Chris Adamou made up the party. Jack was a chemist and he wanted to get some special medicine. He couldn't get what he wanted, as the chemists up there wouldn't let him have whatever it was, so he had to go back to his own dispensary.

"Secondly, one morning, Enoeda *Sensei* came into the dormitory with a billiard cue. He was practising focussing with it. He slowly brought it over his head, holding the thin end with both hands, and stopping it in front of his chest. He practised this a few times and then he did the same action, but quickly, and he snapped the cue in two. That's fantastic focus, sheer *kime*.

"Talking of wood, I went into the manufacturing of *makiwara* with Chris Adamou. Kanazawa *Sensei* helped us on that and another venture, and on one occasion loaned us the money to get started – about two hundred pounds I believe, which was a lot of money in those days. Chris and I were happy-go-lucky lads, carefree, disorganized, living from day to day, and Kanazawa said that we would have to structure ourselves if we were going into business. He had a degree in economics, so we listened. He said, "Oh! Mr. Randly. You will have to write a schedule for the whole day and tick off as you complete each task." That was good advice, and it worked for us.

"We made and sold the *makiwara* through a company we set up called Hiraku Importing, which had an oak leaf logo, upon which was a rising sun badge. It looked really nice, and on each *makiwara*

Master Kanazawa and Nick Adamou square up for *kumite*.

Master Kanazawa on the Hiraku *makiwara*

there was a gold sticker which read: "This Hiraku product has been tested and is recommended by Hirokazu Kanazawa," and then followed Kanazawa's signature. With each *makiwara* came a four page pamphlet, "The Reasons and Needs for Using a MK1-69 Makiwara", which I think we wrote and Kanazawa put his name to.

"The *makiwara* was set onto a large wooden base and supported by a triangular metal frame. The frame was set just over ninety degrees, because the ash blade would bend with use, and this obtuse angle prevented this happening. In fact, we made two blades. The first was thicker and had a soft striking pad, and was intended for the beginner, as it was considered ideal for learning to feel one's own muscle tension. The thin blade with the hard rubber striking pad, was for the more advanced student, and was designed for training in speed and *kime*. For kicking techniques, the thicker *makiwara* was recommended, irrespective of level of expertise, but the thinner blade could be used for snap-kicks.

"Later, the Adamou brothers and I went to Cologne with a few of these *makiwara* strapped to a roof rack. That was quite a little adventure actually."

Nick Adamou remembers the trip well, and a freestyle encounter that Michael had with a German karateka, so: "We were in Nagai *Sensei's dojo* in Dusseldorf ... Kanazawa *Sensei* asked all of us to do freestyle and Mick paired up with this large German. In an instant, Mick scored against him with a powerful technique. I remember being amazed at the speed and precision of Mick's technique and how decisive it was."

Michael continued: "After I completed my apprenticeship as a carpenter and joiner, I went to work for Alan Clemens, who owned a small electrical retail business, in Hackney. I worked behind the counter, making up electrical fittings such as fluorescent lamps, and so on. Clemens, you may recall, was one of the beginners I had taught up on the stage at Blackfriars. I learned after that lesson that Alan lived very near to me and he offered to drive me home. He had a car, and that was quite unusual in those days. I was senior in karate to Alan of course, and he asked me to teach him when we had any spare time, which I was pleased to do, for I was getting extra training in myself.

"Above the shop, there was an empty floor, and he converted it into a *dojo*. It had a speedball, a long mirror, a *makiwara*, and so on. It was well kitted out, and Kanazawa would come along and give Alan private lessons too. *Sensei* would turn up with his karate *gi* on under his overcoat or mackintosh. One of the most impressive feats I ever saw Kanazawa perform happened in that little *dojo*, and only Alan and I were witnesses to it. I don't think the story has been told before.

"Kanazawa was teaching Clemens *gohon-kumite*. Alan was moving forward, attacking *jodan oi-zuki*, and Kanazawa was stepping back, blocking *age-uke*. On the last of the five steps – remember this was at full speed and Alan was a big man – Kanazawa slid back into a *zenkutsu-dachi*, blocked, and countered *gyaku-zuki*, in the traditional way. However, I noticed that Kanazawa's back leg wasn't completely straight and his heel wasn't touching the floor, which was very odd. I looked closer and saw that something was under his back foot. *Sensei* lifted his foot and there, under it, unbroken, was a light bulb. Alan and I had changed the bulb before *Sensei* had arrived, and had inadvertantly left it on the floor near the wall. *Sensei* had, incredibly, slid back into the stance, put the ball of his back foot down first, felt something underfoot, and not placed his heel down. That was truly remarkable, unbelievable actually, yet I can assure you that it's quite true. Imagine the speed of reflex required to be able to do that? Is it any wonder that we were in awe of the man!

"We used to have parties in that *dojo*. These were men's parties – no women. *Sensei* didn't encourage us to have girlfriends really.

Nick Adamou, Chris Adamou and Michael Randall perform *yoko-geri kekomi*.

Karate came first. Some of us did have girlfriends of course, and *Sensei* certainly had an eye for the girls. He was able to attract the women easily.

"I used to play in a band before I started karate, playing rhythm guitar, and at one of the karate parties, a nice big party, we had a band revival. I was playing in front of *Sensei* and the other lads. It was quite embarrassing really, and I'm glad I only had to do it the once. We just played pop really; it was all electric instruments, apart from the drums of course. There was one particular tune, I think it's called *Nagasaki*, an instrumental, that Kanazawa liked, and we played it for him. We used to play quite a few of The Shadows instrumentals, and a favourite was *Apache*. One of the other members of that band was Mervyn, who played lead guitar. I've mentioned him before.

"Eddie Whitcher graded to 2nd Dan along with Andy Sherry and Jack Green just before the 1967 KUGB Championships. They were the top British Shotokan grades in the country, along with Charles Mack, who was actually the senior. A few weeks later, Eddie and Mick Peachey set off on their long time planned trip to Japan. I went to see them off at Liverpool Street Station with Chris and Nick. That was in August, 1967. They were going overland to Japan, as it were, via the Trans-Siberian Railway. Eddie and Mick had planned to fly

The late, great, Eddie Whitcher

out to Tokyo originally, but the Trans-Siberian Railway trip was a lot cheaper, and it was in the days before it was modernised. Flying at that time was very expensive, and none of us had any money.

"I was deeply saddened, heart-broken in fact, that I couldn't go with them, but family responsibilities prevented me from taking part in what, I'm sure, would have been a great adventure. However, later on I did train in Japan. Actually, I felt doubly gutted at their parting, because I was losing two of my best buddies. Eddie stayed out there four years and became the first British man to grade to 3rd Dan at the JKA, which was a hell of an achievement. That was under Nakayama. Mick Peachey stayed out there for five years, I think, and learned to speak fluent Japanese. He graded to 2nd Dan. They both had a very hard time of it at the JKA headquarters, I can tell you. Eddie used to tell me about his freestyle encounters with Yano, or "The Animal", as the westerns used to call him. Because Eddie was so tall, it seemed that every JKA instructor wanted to pair up with him, frequently, to see if their techniques worked! He fought the best the JKA could throw at him – greats like Takeshi Oishi and Hiroshi Shoji. Both Eddie and Mick saw it through though, and that is a testament to the early BKF training and Kanazawa's teaching.

"When Eddie came back, he was sharp, very sharp, absolutely first-rate, the best in the country for my money. He was a big man and yet his techniques were fast and crisp. He had real *kime* – no question about it. You could hear every sinew working a good distance away when he performed *kata*. You couldn't really get near him in freestyle. He had great reach with those long arms and legs, and they would come up on you from nowhere. A great karateka and a very dear friend. I didn't know what to say when he died. I was just numbed by it. Who would have thought that a man like that would have died of cancer at forty-nine? If there's a God out there, I sure hope he knows what he's doing.

"After they left for Japan, I thought that even though I couldn't go, I could still do my best to train like them. I thought, "Well, I know they will sleep on the floor," so the first thing that went was the bed. I put down a sheet of polythene on the lino, which covered the concrete floor, and put a sleeping bag over me. I wanted to try these Spartan conditions to see if it would toughen me up, and I think it did. I slept like that for about three months, but I ended up with bad back aches and that interfered with my training, so although the exercise was hardening me up spiritually, it wasn't doing my body any good.

"I also stepped my training up, and I practised every single day, without exception. Alan Clemens would come and collect me each morning at 6.00 am. I'd be waiting in my karate *gi*, and we'd go over to the park, London Fields, in Hackney, and train for about half an hour in really hard basics, non stop, and then he'd drive me home and I'd have a stone cold bath. The reason why I did this was because I'd read Oyama's book, where he was sitting under a waterfall. Now, there aren't any scenic waterfalls in Hackney, so I thought a cold

Masters Shiro Asano, Hirokazu Kanazawa and Sadashige Kato awaiting their flight at Heathrow Airport.

bath might somehow achieve the same results. The cold baths also went on for quite a few months. It was something I felt that I wanted to do, to compensate for not going to Japan. I didn't want to lose any "distance." I wanted to be able to keep up with Eddie and Mick when they returned. If they gained something, and I was sure that they would, I wanted it as well. Although I did write to Eddie and Mick whilst they were in Japan, and they wrote back, I was not a great letter writer, and Eddie wrote mostly to his parents, and Mick wrote mostly to the Adamou brothers.

"The early morning training in the park went on for years. After training, I'd have a hearty breakfast and set off for work. When I got home, I'd go training in the evenings with Kanazawa. That was my life.

"My training during that period was very intense and I really

Michael performing *tameshiwari* at the Winchmore Hill *dojo*.

couldn't have trained any harder. It gave me a certain sharpness of awareness. I'll give you an example of what I mean. One night, I was asleep on the floor, and behind me was a wardrobe. On top of the wardrobe was a large paper carrier bag jammed full of crockery. In the middle of the night, whilst asleep on my back, I heard the crinkly sound of the bag moving and then for a split second, silence.

As fast as lightning, I rolled over, and the heavily laden bag crashed down to the floor. I got up, turned the light on with a *mawashi-geri*, my usual trick, and the plates and dishes were smashed on the exact spot where my head had been whilst I was asleep a few seconds before.

"I used to walk along at night, in those days, after training, and be able to sense when I was being observed. I did that many times, and the culprits were always cats. Sometimes I couldn't see them, but I knew they were there, and I'd flush them out of the bushes. I had that sixth sense for a long time. I believe that ability came about as a result of the intensive training. A heightened awareness I suppose you'd call it. I haven't got that today, but it's not really possible to keep that type of training up as you get older. Now, I believe, it's more age and experience – what's that person thinking?

"I'm so pleased that I was able to experience that type of thing, and so much more, and I have Kanazawa *Sensei* largely to thank for that. He inspired me. He trained me in the way of Karate-do. He educated me in the way of life, through karate. Although it was Vernon Bell, Jimmy Neal and Terry Wingrove that provided the basis for my karate training and, make no mistake, I shall always be deeply grateful to them for that, it was Kanazawa *Sensei* who completely changed my life.

"The training was very hard in those days, gruelling, but you got something deep from that. Nowadays, it just isn't the same, although I personally do my best to keep it so. Business has crept in and generally the money's the important thing, not the real karate. The wide-boys and entrepreneurs have largely taken over, believe me, and now the punter gets what the punter wants – what the punter expects. To see *real* karate practised these days is, in my opinion, quite a rare thing. But it's still out there, clinging on by the finger-tips, in the odd little *dojo*. Perhaps it was always like that? It's not so much a question of technique, it never was, but more one of personal commitment by instructors and students alike. Real karate shouldn't be viewed as a hobby, as a recreational pastime, that's one of the things that degrades it.

"When Kanazawa finally departed from these shores for Germany, the London *dojo* were lost once again, really. I had trained with him virtually every day for more than three years. He had been my guiding light, my teacher, my mentor. I suppose he thought that we could now make it standing on our own feet – I don't know? Nick and Chris Adamou, Ray Fuller and I would receive our 2nd Dans shortly,

From left to right: Nick Adamou, Chris Adamou, Master Kanazawa, Michael Randall and unknown karateka, at the Winchmore Hill *dojo*

so I reckon we had a reasonable understanding, technically speaking, of what we were doing. Ray ran the Blackfriars *dojo* with Pauline, and Nick, Chris and I had two *dojo*. The first was at the Ross Wyld Hall in Walthamstow, which we changed to the YMCA, in Walthamstow, and the second was at the Winchmore Hill Secondary School, and opposite at the Winchmore Hill Primary School, in Highfield Road. We lost the primary school, but my *dojo* is still based at the Secondary School. I believe it to be the oldest *dojo* in North London where karate has been continuously practised [since 1968].

"Nick, Chris and I continued to train and teach in the manner laid down by Kanazawa after he'd left, for we wanted to keep the spirit of what had been imparted to us intact and alive. All three of us felt that to be important. Later still, we too went our own ways. However, although many years and many miles may now be between us, there is a bond there that can never be broken, for it was forged out of the blood, sweat and tears of that early karate training. In the same way, Eddie Whitcher stills lives in my mind. Death has not really separated us. I can still feel the power of his techiques and his warm friendship. The impression he left was a lasting one.

"And of Kanazawa *Sensei*? What can I say? He is a great man with an important mission in life. The Fates were kind enough to allow me the good fortune of starting karate when I did, and, later, to become such a close student of his during this influential period. But of course it wasn't just good fortune, for I had dedication and I had purpose. I persevered when times were difficult and I never gave up. I suppose that must be one of the secrets of karate? Kanazawa responded, and, as a consequence, he enriched my life beyond all measure. He taught me not only the techniques of Shotokan, but also pointed a way, by example, of how to live through the art of Karate-do. It hasn't been easy at times to stick to this path, it hasn't been easy at all, but that, beyond all else, is what I have to chiefly thank him for."

VI

THE KANAZAWA LEGACY – A VERY PERSONAL VIEW

Part I

Michael Randall continued: "Kanazawa *Sensei* would return to Britain normally about once a year to take classes, after he'd left, and he would always come to the Winchmore Hill *dojo*. He stayed at my house, as did the other instructors Kanazawa brought with him. They used to call my house the Randly Hotel. When *Sensei* came on his own, it was a lot easier for us to cope, but on some occasions we had four, five, and even six instructors staying. It was pretty cramped I can tell you, because I've only got a small house, and there were camp beds all over the place. We would have a great time entertaining them though, and they were marvellous company. My wife, who took time off work, would act as translator when things were unclear, and she ensured that they all had what they wanted. I learned a tremendous amount from the instructors on these occasions, most notably how the Japanese mind works. Understanding that mind helped me enormously, not only in my karate, but in my approach to daily life as well.

"I remember on one occasion, when *Sensei* went to the loo, that I could hear strange clicking sounds coming from behind the bathroom door at the top of the stairs. I wondered what on earth it could be, as I had never heard clicks coming from the toilet before. This sound went on for quite some time and I became rather concerned. I needn't have worried however, for after *Sensei* emerged, *nunchaku* in hand, I realised that he'd been practising. He then told me that he was due to give a *nunchaku* demonstration at Crystal Palace in the near future.

"Kanazawa's demonstration went brilliantly. I'm tired of trying to think up superlatives to describe him; "brilliant" will have to do! Half-way through his routine, he jumped high into the air whilst

Training at the Winchmore Hill *dojo* under Master Kato – 1973.

performing a 360 degree turn, and as he did so, one of his fellowinstructors threw an apple at him, which *Sensei* struck with the *nunchaku*, smashing it into tiny pieces. This truly magnificent piece of timing and distancing was performed in the wink of an eye. I thought that was incredible. Imagine having the expertise, the confidence, to perform that feat in front of so many spectators. You

Training at the Winchmore Hill dojo under Master Kanazawa - 1973.

have to marvel, really. He then landed in a stance and continued his demonstration. Kanazawa later wrote a book entitled, *Nunchaku Dynamic Training*, and believe me, Kanazawa's *nunchaku* is dynamic!

"When *Sensei* ate a meal at the Randly Hotel, he never seemed to eat a large one. I asked him about this, and he told me that one should always leave the table feeling a little hungry, for it is much healthier that way.

"On another occasion, Kanazawa brought four or five junior instructors with him. There was a 4th Dan and the rest were 3rd Dans, and they were all about my age at the time. That evening, they came to my *dojo* with *Sensei* to train. It was a good lesson and at the end we practised freestyle with them. They were all very good. One of my students was a 4th Dan in judo, and if he ever got close enough to throw you, he would. He paired up with one of the Japanese instructors, and during an exchange of various techniques, he managed to sweep the Japanese over and put some kind of lock on him. After a few seconds, the Japanese slapped the floor, to show that he had submitted. After that, they squared up again, and I wondered what would happen next. I should have guessed! At about

Master Kanazawa and Robert Randall (who reached the grade of 2nd kyu).

twice the speed of an Exocet missile, the Japanese was on him. Down went my student, and the Japanese was on him with a strangle hold. It was then the turn of my student to slap the floor for all he was worth. That little incident taught me a lesson; one should always be on guard. Although the Japanese instructor was far superior in technique, I suspect that he had just dropped his guard for a moment.

"Kanazawa once brought his elder brother over to Britain. They didn't stay at the Randly Hotel on that occasion, but at a hotel in London. The brother was a nice man, very quiet and humble. He was, I think, quite wealthy, for he owned a fishing fleet. Asano *Sensei* married his daughter.

"In 1970, when I was a 2nd Dan, I was chosen to be a member of a British Shotokan karate team to take on a Japanese combined universities all-styles team, at Crystal Palace. You may not believe this, but I can't remember much about the event. Competition has never interested me, as I've said before. I recall snippets, such as Kato *Sensei* lent me his *gi* for the tournament, but I can not for the life of me remember why, though I think I may have left mine at home! I seem to recall that I went up for my bout in the middle of the competition, and scored against my opponent, a big man, with a *gyaku-zuki*, and received a *wazari* [half-point]. He then scored on me with a punch, to even things up, and then got another half-point, with a punch, to win. The late Steve Cattle was in the British team too. I remember him flying forward punching, and *kiai'ing* for all he was worth. Terry O'Neill was there as well, and he performed a wonderful *gyaku-mawashi-geri* on his opponent, but didn't even receive a half-point. I couldn't believe it. He should have received an *ippon* [full-point] in my opinion. The judging seemed to be very curious that day. The British team lost.

"Speaking of teams, after winning the world karate championships, in Paris [in 1972], members of the Japanese squad visited England before returning home. As usual, Kanazawa *Sensei*, who had acted as coach to the Japanese team, and now held the rank of 7th Dan, visited the Winchmore Hill *dojo* with Asano *Sensei* and Kato *Sensei*. The members of the victorious JKA squad who accompanied them that evening were, Masahiko Tanaka, Yoshiharu Osaka and Mikio Yahara. Osaka and Yahara looked to be in their mid twenties, and Tanaka about thirty years old. The lesson began with a warm-up session, which Kanazawa took, and then he instructed us in basics. After that, we all sat down along the edge of the *dojo*, while Tanaka, Osaka and Yahara called us up to pair with them in

Michael, as part of the British team, about to face his JKA team opponent –
Crystal Palace, 1970.

gohon-kumite. They were superb. I paired up with Tanaka *Sensei*.
Tanaka's *oi-zuki* was something to behold. We practised *chudan*. I
think he caught me three out of the five punches; I was unable to
catch him even once.

"We all then sat down in a large circle and were invited to pair up
with one of the team for freestyle. I think Chris Adamou got up first.
Kanazawa *Sensei* selected Yahara, who is noted for his awesome
fighting spirit, to act as his opponent. Yahara was a student of Kenji
Yano, who Eddie came across in Japan, much to his regret, as I've
mentioned, and I remember reading that in the Paris championships,
Yahara had performed a spectacular back somersault to escape from
danger. He was also a gifted thrower. We all sat up straight, fully
attentive, to await the action. We didn't have to wait very long!

"Chris and Yahara squared up to one another, Kanazawa said,
"Hajime!", and before you could count to two, Chris was laid out
flat on his back by Yahara's famous *mawashi-geri*. It was so fast that
none of us really saw it. It was devastating. Kanazawa said something
to Yahara in Japanese, and I think that he was telling him to ease off
a bit.

"One of the next to get up was a student of mine, Greg Durant.

Michael's Great Britain team badge

He enjoyed a bit of freestyle, but before you could blink an eye, SMACK! Yahara's *mawashi-geri* was there again, like grease lightning. Greg collapsed – whoomp! I felt sorry for him, because I hadn't expected him to try his luck.

"By now, we were all seriously contemplating who would be next, but I don't recall Yahara flooring anyone else. Yahara, of course, competed magnificently, for many years, in the JKA Championships' individual *kumite* event, and although he came very close a number of times, he never won it. He did, however, take the JKA individual *kata* title in 1984, performing *Unsu*. Yahara has that very rare ability to appear to be able to hover during the 360 degree jump in that *kata* – it's weird.

"After Kanazawa told Yahara to sit down, he called up Osaka *Sensei*. I then decided to get up. I thought I may as well have a go. What did I have to lose? – only my conscious state! I had an injury to my leg and was hobbling a bit. Osaka must have noticed this and seemed to take it easy with me. He didn't floor anybody, but he was every bit as good as Yahara, and of course went on to win the JKA individual *kumite* title four years later. After I sat down, I felt really proud that I had fought a world karate champion. After all, it's not every day you can say that!

"Finally, Kanazawa *Sensei* called up Tanaka, and he looked every

From left to right: Michael Nursey, Nicholas Adamou, Christopher Adamou, Masahiko Tanaka, Roger Hall, Mikio Yahara, Michael Randall and John Alcock – 1972

inch as good as the other two. His control was excellent and his timing impeccable. He was tremendously powerful. Tanaka took the JKA individual *kumite* title in 1974 and 1975, and won the individual world championship *kumite* title in 1977, as well. So these men were real individual champions, of the highest order, in the making, and today are household names in the Shotokan world. Of course, as I've said, they were world team champions at the time, and believe me, they were exceptionally good.

"When the Dan grades who had wanted to have a turn had done so, Kanazawa then called up Yahara, Tanaka and Osaka to practise freestyle with one another. What we saw then was surely one of the most awesome displays of freestyle ever given in this country, or anywhere else come to that. They were like Siberian tigers fighting – so fast – and yet each technique was executed to perfection, or close to it.

"To conclude the display, Kanazawa *Sensei* asked Osaka to demonstrate a *kata*. Osaka *Sensei* chose *Jion*. Osaka, of course, went on to take the JKA individual *kata* title a record six times, in consecutive years [1978-1983]. He also won the World Karate

A group shot of the Winchmore Hill *dojo* on the occasion of the visit of Masters Yahara, Tanaka, Asano, Kanazawa, Kato and Osaka – 1972.

Championships *kata* title in 1977. I think that on that evening, Osaka's *Jion* almost equalled Kanazawa's *kata*. It really was that good. It was like watching poetry in motion.

"After the lesson had finished, we all went to a club house that we used for socialising. We also used it for giving students private lessons, and Kanazawa sometimes gave the odd private lesson there too. As the club house was often frequented by Kanazawa – it was here that he would invariably give us talks on his personal philosophy of karate – and as the majority of the other Japanese instructors visited there over the years, it was consequently named, "The In-depth Society." We had our own licensed bar and we were able to bring in food, so that evening was indeed memorable.

"Eddie, Nick and Chris Adamou, and I, left the KUGB and joined Kanazawa's newly formed Shotokan Karate International. That must have been around 1973, when the four of us were 3rd Dans. SKI was, I believe, the international section of the JKA when it was first formed, but it became a separate organization, distinct from the JKA, in 1977, with Kanazawa as the Chief Instructor. During the early to mid Seventies, Asano *Sensei* would drive down from his base in Nottingham and teach at the Winchmore club every fortnight, on a Friday evening, and stay over at the Randly Hotel. These sessions were pretty gruelling. Towards the end of the lesson, Asano, who was a past All Japan University Champion – very tough – would freestyle with all the black-belts, one at a time, and sometimes the brown-belts as well. We were all kicked around you might say, and I had my share of bloody noses. Sometimes Kato *Sensei* would visit.

"In 1976, I was appointed team coach for the SKI, which I have always considered a great honour. I'm not quite sure why Asano *Sensei* chose me, but it may have been because he had made me

Master Kanazawa and Michael outside The Clubhouse – the In-depth Society.

A group shot of famous instructors (1974 to 1978). From left to right, standing: Chris Adamou, Nick Adamou, Will Mannion, Master Asano, Paul Perry, Master Kanazawa, Eddie Whitcher, Michael Randall, Peter Videan, Harry Jones; kneeling: Mick Nursey, John Alcock, Roger Hall, unknown.

London Area Chief Karate Instructor for SKI

Michael's SKI licence showing his 1st, 2nd and 3rd Dan grading dates

London Area Chief Instructor. Asano and I got on very well. He seemed to either like you, or not. He was one of the few Japanese *Sensei* who would tell you exactly what he thought. He never minced his words, and you knew exactly where you stood with him. We all respected Asano for that. Of course, his karate was fantastic. He had lovely timing – so relaxed, so fluent.

"As SKI team coach, the squad and I went to Japan with a view to take part in the JKA Championships that year. Eddie Whitcher and I were the only members representing the south of England, for all the others were from the Midlands or up north. The team were one of the very first group of passengers to fly to Japan via the North Pole. We flew JAL – Japan Airlines. The service provided by the airline and crew was really first-rate and equal to any five-star hotel. We flew by jumbo jet, which was really novel in those days. I can remember being quite overwhelmed by the plane's size. We had one short stop-over in Anchorage, Alaska.

"We trained in Gifu and Kyoto. The *dojo* were very small compared to ours in the West, and we trained so closely next to one another that we couldn't practise *mawashi-geri* properly. The training was hard, repetitious, and very spirited. The Japanese had a great sense of camaraderie going, and when some of them were seated on the floor during *kumite* practice – there just wasn't enough room for all the students to practise *jiyu-ippon* at once – they would yell words of encouragement to their fellow karateka, which was strange, as we didn't do anything like that in Britain. Because it was the rainy season when we visited Japan, our karate *gi* would get so wet with sweat, because of the heat and humidity, that we could virtually wring them out at the end of a lesson. We never trained in *kata* the whole time we were there, which I thought was a little surprising. I didn't see any older people training, and throughout our entire stay I never once saw a woman in a karate *gi*.

"There were just two belt colours in operation – white and black. Before I knew this, I partnered a white-belt who was unbelievably good. He was fast and sharp, and I thought to myself, "My God! If this is what the beginners are like over here, what can the black-belts do?" The student in question was a 1st kyu however, and about to take his Dan grade shortly. When I found that out, it put my mind at rest!

"We travelled to —— in the bullet train, and it was there, quite unexpectedly, that I had one of the most unusual experiences one could possibly imagine – an evening with the *yakuza* [Japanese gangsters]. I want to make it quite clear that this incident [a description of which follows shortly] had absolutely nothing to do with Kanazawa *Sensei* or SKI in any way. Kanazawa wasn't even with us at the time. It was an 'extra curricular' social event. I tell the anecdote solely because it happened to me as a result of my karate, in that I wouldn't have gone to Japan save for my karate. I also like to think that it's a good story!

"When we arrived at our station, we were greeted by a group of karateka and an instructor. The students were all quite young, mostly in their twenties, I should imagine. We were ushered into cars and, at a rate of knots, sped off. We drove for quite some time, and as we were driving along the suburban roads, we could see policeman in rigid poses. As we passed these policeman, we realised that they were made of plastic. Eddie and I thought that this was hilarious. It was explained to us that whilst driving, it is difficult to recognise the real thing from the unreal, because of the speed being travelled. The idea of the plastic policeman, and they were realistic, was to deter speeding motorists. Apparently, the police would come along from time to time and move these dummies to different locations in order to fox motorists. They also sometimes substituted the dummy for the real thing! Our companions said that irate motorists often stole the dummies and disposed of them in less than dignified ways.

"Our destination was a fish restaurant, and it was owned by the father of one of the student karateka we were with. The entire restaurant had been booked for us. Upon each table were the most beautiful displays of food, one portion laid out for each guest. It was like a work of art. Each person had before them what looked like a glass gondola, which was filled to the brim with raw fish of different kinds. The dish is called *sashimi*.

"After we sat down, beer and steaming hot boiled rice was brought. The meal must have taken many hours to prepare. I recently checked prices at various Japanese restaurants, and a meal like that today would cost in excess of £100 per head. I was hungry and tucked in immediately. I had never eaten raw fish before, but I had sampled smoked salmon and jellied eels. I thoroughly enjoyed the dinner, and it has since become one of my favourite meals. When I looked around however, I was amazed to see that none of the other English lads were eating. They just turned up their noses and drank the beer. Indeed, they wouldn't even try the meal. It was really embarrassing. Japanese people love to show their hospitality, and we, as a group, showed absolutely no appreciation for all the effort they had made.

No wonder many foreigners think that the Brits are just football hooligans and lager louts.

"On another occasion, in Tokyo, we went to the Ginza, which is equivalent to Oxford Street, in London, and a Japanese friend of Eddie's, who owned a cafe, took the British team out for a meal at a top night club. The bill came to over two hundred pounds, then! He insisted on paying, yet he only knew Eddie. The Japanese hospitality is second to none. They can be such warm people. I think that we English could learn a lesson from them.

"Anyway, after the *sashimi*, we were taken to a plush hotel and shown our rooms. All our travelling and accommodation fees had been paid for, and we only had to find our spending money. Eddie and I were given a room to share, which was kitted out with every mod-con. After a short while, there was a loud banging on the door, accompanied by the words, "Going! Going!" We were to hear this numerous times during our stay. Although very tired by now, and just wanting to catch forty winks, when you heard "Going! Going!" you just had to go, for it was ——— *Sensei*.

"We all assembled in the downstairs lounge. ——— *Sensei* had booked, for our exclusive use, the natural spring bath in the basement. It was very strange, even surreal, for under the hotel was a very large bath, marble I believe, much bigger than a rugby team's bath, circular in shape, and full to the brim with cloudy, very hot water. Apparently, the water contained many minerals and salts that were efficacious to health. One of the team, a bit of a Jack-the-lad, stripped off his *yukata* and dived straight in. This is how we learned the water was hot! You have never seen anyone swim so quickly; Mark Spitz [the famous Olympic swimmer who won nine gold medals] would have been impressed. The water was so hot that this chap couldn't get to the other side fast enough. When he emerged, he looked like a scolded lobster, and his eyes looked as though they were sticking out on stalks. He just sat on the side afterwards. The wind had been taken completely out of his sails alright!

"The next evening, we were invited to the house of a very senior *yakuza*, whose name was ——— . He was the top man for this part of Japan, and he invited us to his house so that he could talk about ——— [not a karate instructor], who was coming to England. We took a cab, which drew up outside this rather impressive residence. We were then shown into a large room, which was narrow, but long. I am told that most *yakuza* have a room like this in their houses. Running the entire length of this room, in the centre, were very low wooden tables, joined together. The tables were fully laden with food of every description. I could see at once that the food was very expensive. There was also an unbelievable amount of alcohol. I remembered coming through customs at Hanada Airport and a bottle of Napoleon Brandy cost a fortune, and here there were bottles of it everywhere. No expense had been spared.

"After we had exchanged introductions, we sat down on the floor, crossed-legged, on cushions, and were invited to eat and drink. The evening began in a very convivial mood, but that mood didn't last too long.

"You never pour your own drink on such occasions in Japan, as this would deprive the host of the honour of pouring it for you. When a drink is poured for you, you must drink all that is in your glass before accepting any more. As ——*Sensei* explained to us, to refuse to drink would be considered an insult, as it meant that you were refusing your host's hospitality. If you were not a drinker, then that was most unfortunate, especially as the measures poured were, with no exaggeration, equal to at least five whiskies. You had to hold your glass up to be refilled. It is considered an insult not to hold the glass up. If, when you are asked to take another drink, you just point to your glass on the table, that indicates that the person pouring is your servant.

"All the *yakuza* present were tattooed, and this tattooing had been paid for by —— [the *oyabun*, or boss]. Each tattoo – which appeared most notably on their backs, and invariably depicted a samurai warrior - might be considered a work of art, and costs literally thousands of pounds. The *yakuza* will only show you their tattoos if requested to do so by a senior *yakuza*. It is regarded as an honour to see such a tattoo, and one is expected to show great awe; not to do so would be taken as an insult.

"During the course of the evening, one of the senior *yakuza* asked a junior to show us his tattoo. It was quite clear that the junior didn't want to, though eventually he did show us. When he finally removed the top of his clothing, we could see why they were so expensive. Across the whole top of his back was a samurai warrior in full armour, brandishing a sword in a hostile manner. It really was very impressive. The colours looked so real, so vivid, and the detail was incredible. I understand that such tattoos can only be done by the Japanese. I remember saying, *"Arigato! Arigato!"*, which is Japanese for, "Thank you! Thank you!"

"The apprentice *yakuza*, or *koban*, are indebted to their boss for paying for their tattoos and, if they ever want to leave his service, are obliged to chop off their little finger and give it to him as a means of redemption for their debt.

"Anyway, the evening progressed, and then for no apparent reason, all the guests were asked to stand and raise their glasses and drink a series of toasts to —— [the boss]. We had to stand and hold our glasses at arm's length whilst pointing them at —— [the boss] and shout "——" [the name of the boss]. We then had to empty our glasses before we resumed the sitting position. We didn't have a clue why we were obliged to just stand up like that, out of the blue, and drink so many toasts, but a few hours on, and many more drinks later, we asked, "What were the toasts for?" We were calmly told that each toast was for a person that —— [the boss] had ordered assassinated!

"As you can imagine, when we heard this, we became concerned for our own safety. Each of the *yakuza* carried a samurai sword – we didn't see any guns, but I bet they weren't too far away – and as the evening wore on, and as the drinks flowed, the voices of the *yakuza* became raised almost to shouting pitch. Although the proceedings didn't become too rowdy, I felt that the atmosphere definitely became a bit tense at times, and you could say that we distinctly minded our P's and Q's! I remember that one of the Japanese karate instructors, whose name I cannot recall, with whom I had been having a very polite and agreeable conversation earlier on in the evening, had become rather drunk, and for no reason at all, grabbed a pair of chopsticks and glared at me from across the table and said, "I will break your ribs like this!" and broke the chopsticks in my face. Well, what do you do in such circumstances? I suspected that he had drunk far more than he could handle. So, to diffuse the situation, I tried to look as calm as possible, and slowly bowed and quietly said, *"Oss ... Oss."* This seemed to have the desired effect, and his attention was then drawn to something else.

"—— [the boss] sat in the corner, so no one could approach him from behind, I suspect. He acted in a very humble manner, as it is considered vulgar to be self-important. —— *Sensei* asked him to come and sit with us at the table, but he refused. After many requests, and many refusals, —— *Sensei* went over and almost lifted him up from his seat to join us. Without doubt, —— [the boss] just didn't want to look pompous. That may have been so, but that didn't fool anyone for a single minute. To reach the position this man had achieved in the Japanese underworld, he must have been absolutely ruthless.

"The next day, back at our hotel, we were all the worse for wear, but it had been a very interesting experience and I wouldn't have missed it. Who would have thought that we would have been the guests of a top *yakuza*? When I look back, my thoughts are clouded with nostalgia and emotion, and I realise just how much I miss Eddie [who was also at the dinner]. If only one percent of karateka could even try to be like Eddie was, the world of karate would be a much better place today.

"When we went to Tokyo, we stayed with Norihiko Lida *Sensei* and his family. They were lovely people. Lida's karate was exceptionally good. His wife took great care of us, and considering they housed both the British and German teams at the same time, she did a remarkable job. Lida's father was a priest, and the house we stayed in was next to a temple, which was separated from the house by sliding doors. In the morning, when we woke, we could hear the gong being struck in the temple and it gave us a wonderful feeling of being in the Orient.

"Lida *Sensei* had a *dojo* built on top of the house and temple, and this is where, in futons, the two teams slept on the floor. The futons were kept tucked away in cupboards during the day and brought out only at night. One of the students seemed to live in the *dojo* and he had a small area about the size of a small cupboard where he slept and kept his things. When we arrived back at the *dojo* in the evening, invariably after many bouts of *Campai!* – the Japanese equivalent to "Cheers!" – this student insisted that we drank with him. We really did have to be troupers in those days!

"The 1976 Japan Karate Association Championships were a very grand affair. They were held at the Nippon Budokan, a huge stadium, in front of many thousands of spectators on the 19th and 20th June. I think there were eight contest areas, if I remember correctly. I recall that there was a large group of majorettes which, to me at least, seemed out of place at such an event. Unfortunately, the SKI team were not allowed to compete as Enoeda *Sensei* had brought the official team from England, and only one team was allowed to compete from each country. The SKI team were extremely disappointed, as you can imagine, for they had really prepared for the event. However, there was nothing we could do about it, so we sat and watched the championships, and completely enthralled we were too.

"Osaka, who was a 4th Dan at this time, won the freestyle event. He beat our host, Lida *Sensei*, in the second round with a *kizami-*

zuki, then beat Abe *Sensei* in the third round with a punch and Yahara *Sensei* in the semi-finals with the same technique. Abe really impressed me. He was older than the other competitors, in his mid thirties I should say, but his back-fist was incredibly fast. Osaka had impeccable timing and his hands were like lightning too. In the final, which was refereed by Master Nakayama, Osaka *Sensei* beat Norimasa Hayakawa. It was a three-point/five minute final, and Osaka scored with punches and kicks. I remember that when Nakayama *Sensei* called out *"Hajime!"*, to begin the contest, Hayakawa just stood there, rooted, glaring at Osaka, and let forth with a most tremendous *kiai*. That must have been very unsettling, but Osaka had nerves of steel.

"That *kiai* reminded me of a little story Kanazawa *Sensei* once told me. He said that in times gone by, men used to go into the woods and low mountain pastures and practise *kiai-jitsu*. They would focus these intense, fearful, blood-curdling yells at birds flying over who, frozen with fright on hearing the *kiai*, would fall from the sky.

"Hideo Ochi won the *kata* with a *Nijushiho* which was just out of this world – so fast, so strong; perfect form. He was a 6th Dan at the time. I remember the day after the championships, that Ochi *Sensei*, who I trained under and very much liked, ate a large bowl of mussels for breakfast. He said that they would help him to replenish the energy he had lost during the tournament. All the Japanese I met seemed to like seafood. This was the fifth JKA title Ochi had won, for he had previously been Grand Champion in 1966, taken the individual *kumite* title in 1967 and the individual *kata* title in 1969. Ochi is a superb karateka. Hitoshi Kasuya, another 4th Dan, who later became a top SKI man and Kanazawa's assistant, though I understand he has left that organisation now, came second with a lovely *Kanku-sho*. Takashi Naito, yet another 4th Dan, who later went to Italy for the JKA, came third with the same *kata*.

"Yahara *Sensei* was noted for his fighting spirit, as I have said before. He was awesome in *kumite*, and really extraordinarily inventive, not to say daring. During his quarter-final contest, he was grappling with his opponent, Toshihiro Mori *Sensei*, to avoid being thrown. Mori was a giant of a Japanese, about six foot three inches I would guess. He was much bigger than Yahara and looked as if he practised judo. Yahara, aware that he was about to be thrown, suddenly wrapped his arms around Mori's torso, which, when you think about it, is a clever thing to do in such circumstances. Yahara then, quite unexpectedly, jumped up and appeared to head butt Mori,

Nick Adamou, Chris Adamou, Master Hideo Ochi and Michael Randall

but it all happened so quickly that it was difficult to be certain if the action had been deliberate, or whether Mori had pulled Yahara down onto himself. You could hear the crack of heads all around the Budokan. Mori went out like a light. Master Nishiyama was the referee. To my absolute amazement, the decision went to Yahara, and he went into the semi-finals. [Mori went on to win the JKA individual *kumite* title in 1978, and then again in 1980].

"Another point that I recall about those championships was, whenever a high grade walked past, all the Japanese karateka called out, and in some cases shouted, *"Oss!"* Wherever you were in the Budokan over those two days, you heard *"Oss!"* bellowing.

"Whilst in Tokyo, Eddie and I went to the British Embassy, because Eddie had married a Japanese woman, Toshiko, in Japan, on a previous visit, and had somehow managed to lose the marriage certificate. When we arrived at the embassy, we approached the lift at the same time as another man. He was a typical English gentleman – tall, distinguished, wearing the obligatory thin pencil moustache, collar and tie, pinstripe suit, bowler hat, large dark wool and cashmere overcoat, and carrying a long black umbrella – and very much in the Terry Thomas mould. Remember, this was the rainy season, and I can't imagine how hot and uncomfortable he must have been wearing all those clothes. Eddie and I were wearing *zori* [flip-flops], jeans

175

and open necked shirts, and we were sweltering. The humidity can be pretty awful, and when the rain, which is warm, does fall, there's a deluge.

"As we were going up in the lift, this gentleman made some polite conversation, and he was in fact a very nice person, though somewhat eccentric, I would say. When we got out of the lift, he got out too, and went off. Eddie and I asked directions from a uniformed man and were then ushered into a room, and there was this very English gentleman sitting before us. He introduced us to his second in command, who was Japanese, and very friendly too. The English gentleman instructed his deputy to obtain a duplicate of the marriage certificate, and while this was being done, the Englishman asked us why we were in Japan. We explained that we were with the British karate team, and he congratulated us. When the Japanese came back, the Englishman told his deputy. What happened next was quite extraordinary. The man turned his back on us and cut us off completely. He refused to say anything to us. The Englishman did not quite understand what was going on, and I confess neither did I. After Eddie and I left the building, I asked him the reason for the Japanese man's very negative reaction. Eddie explained that in Japan, the practice of karate is often looked down upon, because it is thought that *yakuza* train in karate. I was very surprised by this answer. I naturally thought that because karate had come from Japan, all Japanese people would understand, and appreciate its merits. Apparently, this is not the case. The Japanese, just like any other people, only know what they are told, so many of those who do not practise karate only have negative thoughts about it. I suppose the position is very similar to the uninformed public's view of karate in Britain forty years ago, when Vernon Bell was trying to establish the art.

"The above incident was not in any way an isolated one. I'll give you another example. Eddie and I were waiting on a platform at a train station, and a very pretty Japanese girl came up to us and enquired if we were English. Although some of the Japanese can speak quite good English, it is American English, and they consider it prestigious to talk to English people. We replied that we were English and that we were in Japan for two weeks. After a short while, she asked us why we were specifically in Japan, and we told her that we were there for the karate tournament. She didn't seem to know what karate was – Eddie said that this was quite common – so we did some chopping motions with our hands. All of a sudden, she realised what we were describing, and promptly turned her back on us and walked away. Eddie and I looked at one another and decided to tell people in the future that we were on holiday. It was a case of being tarred with the same brush. The *yakuza* practise karate, and as we practise karate, we too must be gangsters. That wasn't a nice feeling, for we were proud of what we did.

"When we went to the baths and saw a man with a tattoo on his back, we always gave him a wide berth. —— *Sensei* told me a story once about —— *Sensei* who was at the baths and a man was throwing his weight around, and —— *Sensei* went up to him and promptly floored him. As the man rolled on the tiles, —— *Sensei* saw that an impressive tattoo was on the man's back and, realising what he had done, made a swift exit. To do such a thing would incur the death penalty, I should imagine. The leader of the area's *yakuza* would be informed and, as a matter of honour, revenge would have to be sought. As I understand it, one of the benefits of being a *yakuza* is that your welfare is always taken care of. Well, —— *Sensei* had to lie low for a time whilst complicated negotiations took place. A nasty incident was narrowly avoided.

"Talking of baths, we went to the public baths with Asano *Sensei*. The men were on one side, the women on the other. First you undress and put your clothes in a locker and then you sit on a small seat in front of a tap protruding from the wall. You then wash yourself until you are clean and you finish off by soaking in the communial bath. You never, ever, wash in the bath. One of the fondest habits of the Japanese is to relax in that way. However, a point that we found very odd, was that we paid our fee to a lady who was sitting on a very high seat in the middle of the baths in front of the partition separating the men's and women's sections. She was collecting money from both men and women, and as we were changing and bathing she was watching both males and females. The Japanese seem to accept that as quite normal.

"We had some really funny things happen to us in Japan as well. The manner of dress, some of the customs, and so on, in the Orient, appear strange, not to say bizarre to the western mind. I'll give you a couple of examples. On one occasion, we were walking along a crowded road and a very serious looking man passed us wearing full traditional Japanese dress. Well, that was okay, but what was odd was that he had a model of an old sailing galleon, complete with sails, strapped onto the top of his head. Eddie and I literally just fell about laughing. It was one of the funniest things we had ever seen. I

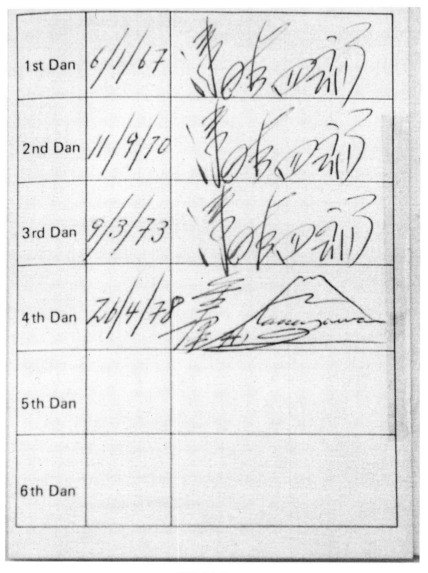

1st Dan	6/1/67	
2nd Dan	11/9/70	
3rd Dan	9/3/73	
4th Dan	26/4/78	
5th Dan		
6th Dan		

SKI 4th Dan

must have nearly burst a blood vessel. But what seemed even funnier, was the fact that all the Japanese people who saw him totally ignored the fact that anything was out of the ordinary. They just stayed poker faced and continued about their business. It really was an hilarious moment.

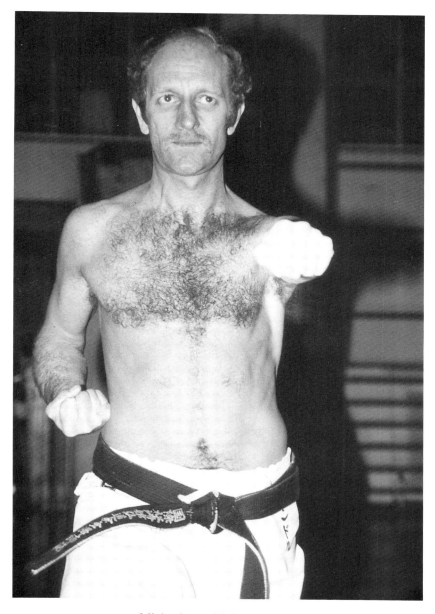

Michael as a 4th Dan – 1978

"In another incident, Eddie and I were told that we should meet Kanazawa *Sensei* outside one of the underground stations. Well, we waited and waited, how long exactly I can't remember, but it must have been three or four hours at least. And then, out of the blue, amongst hundreds of milling people came a cyclist, who was totally unknown to us. As he passed us he shouted, "Kanazawa *Sensei* not coming!" and continued on his way, into the distance, without a single word of explanation. Despite our very long wait, Eddie and I burst into laughter. We both saw the funny side of it.

"Two years later however, back in Britain, Eddie and I, along with John Van Weenen, Roger Hall, Mick Nursey and Harry Jones, amongst others, decided to form our own association, and this we called ESKA – the English Shotokan Karate Association. The whole enterprise was a very big step for us.

"It was a few years after this that Roger Hall and I made the four colour video *Beginner to Black-Belt* tapes. I believe that we were the first in Britain to put Shotokan karate on video, and make it commercially available, through a company we set up called Martial Arts Productions. The tapes, which were on VHS and Betamax formats, were professionally directed by Brian Morton, produced by Roger, and structured using an easy-to-follow, step-by-step approach. That was in 1983, when I was a 5th Dan and Roger was a 4th Dan. The videos were reviewed nationwide, on television, by Adam Faith. Tape I included callisthenics, basic blocks, punches and kicks, multiple self-defence and breaking techniques. Tape II involved intermediate blocks, strikes and kicks, combinations, *ippon-kumite*, knife defence, and the *kata Heian Shodan, Heian Nidan* and *Heian Sandan*, with applications. Tape III contained advanced combinations, *kaeshi-ippon, jiyu-ippon, kata Heian Yondan, Heian Godan* and *Tekki Shodan*, stamina and stretching exercises, and further breaking techniques. Tape IV showed advanced blocks, strikes, stances and kicks, further advanced combinations, more *jiyu-ippon kumite*, the *kata Bassai-dai, Kanku-dai* and *Enpi*, and women's self-defence. We soon realised however, that people copy such tapes, and that you'd sell a set to one club and that was your lot. It was an interesting venture though, and I'm pleased that we did it.

"ESKA was based on very traditional lines, but Eddie left in 1981, losing all interest in karate groups. John Van Weenen followed around 1982 to set up the Traditional Association of Shotokan Karate, and I left in 1984 to help form the Shotokan Karate Association. Karate breeds expansion, for it encourages individual growth, and there were

Michael Randall's Selected Karate Genealogy

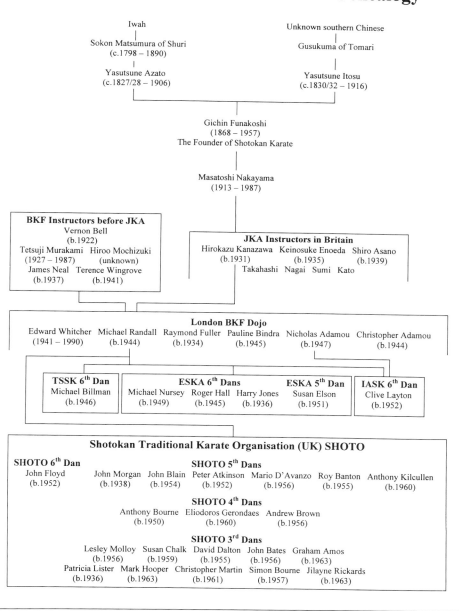

Iwah
|
Sokon Matsumura of Shuri
(c.1798 – 1890)
|
Yasutsune Azato
(c.1827/28 – 1906)

Unknown southern Chinese
|
Gusukuma of Tomari
|
Yasutsune Itosu
(c.1830/32 – 1916)

Gichin Funakoshi
(1868 – 1957)
The Founder of Shotokan Karate

Masatoshi Nakayama
(1913 – 1987)

BKF Instructors before JKA
Vernon Bell
(b.1922)
Tetsuji Murakami   Hiroo Mochizuki
(1927 – 1987)   (unknown)
James Neal   Terence Wingrove
(b.1937)   (b.1941)

JKA Instructors in Britain
Hirokazu Kanazawa   Keinosuke Enoeda   Shiro Asano
(b.1931)   (b.1935)   (b.1939)
Takahashi   Nagai   Sumi   Kato

London BKF Dojo
Edward Whitcher   Michael Randall   Raymond Fuller   Pauline Bindra   Nicholas Adamou   Christopher Adamou
(1941 – 1990)   (b.1944)   (b.1934)   (b.1945)   (b.1947)   (b.1944)

TSSK 6th Dan
Michael Billman
(b.1946)

ESKA 6th Dans
Michael Nursey   Roger Hall   Harry Jones
(b.1949)   (b.1945)   (b.1936)

ESKA 5th Dan
Susan Elson
(b.1951)

IASK 6th Dan
Clive Layton
(b.1952)

Shotokan Traditional Karate Organisation (UK) SHOTO

SHOTO 6th Dan
John Floyd
(b.1952)

SHOTO 5th Dans
John Morgan   John Blain   Peter Atkinson   Mario D'Avanzo   Roy Banton   Anthony Kilcullen
(b.1938)   (b.1954)   (b.1952)   (b.1956)   (b.1955)   (b.1960)

SHOTO 4th Dans
Anthony Bourne   Eliodoros Gerondaes   Andrew Brown
(b.1950)   (b.1960)   (b.1956)

SHOTO 3rd Dans
Lesley Molloy   Susan Chalk   David Dalton   John Bates   Graham Amos
(b.1956)   (b.1959)   (b.1955)   (b.1956)   (b.1963)
Patricia Lister   Mark Hooper   Christopher Martin   Simon Bourne   Jilayne Rickards
(b.1936)   (b.1963)   (b.1961)   (b.1957)   (b.1963)

SHOTO 5th Dan, Roy Banton, attacks *kekomi*, as Michael Randall blocks *ude-uke*.

Some of SHOTO's senior grades – left to right, standing, all 5th Dan: Anthony Kilcullen, Peter Atkinson, John Blain, John Morgan, Mario D'Avanzo; kneeling: Harry Jones (6th Dan ESKA), Michael Randall, John Floyd, 6th Dan.

initially just too many generals in ESKA. Today, that association is very strong indeed, having three 6th Dans – all my students. I'm proud I was a founder of that association.

"I parted as senior instructor to SKA in 1996 and formed the Shotokan Traditional Karate Organisation (UK), which we abbreviate to SHOTO. We are a small, close-knit association, where quality, rather than quantity counts. I like to think that I run this organisation on similar lines to Bell's early BKF, so things have come full circle for me. SHOTO has six 5th Dans, one 6th Dan, and myself as Chief Instructor, so we are very well endowed. I have to listen to all the outside nonsense that's surreptitiously crept into karate, receive all the meaningless admin', but that's a price you pay for being in-charge of an organisation in today's world. I don't think for one minute that Kanazawa would have put up with all the rubbish you get now. He'd just have risen above it, and that's what I try to do. I feel that we have become a nation of accountants, timid little clerks, bureaucrats and legal pen pushers. Who can blame Eddie for walking away? Certainly not I. The word "martial" has generally lost much of its meaning over the last thirty years, in my opinion. Karate seems to have been hamstrung by instructors filling popular demand – out for a quick buck. The prospect of litigation hangs like a cloud over every instructor now, and you have to be seen to be doing what's politically correct. I do my best to keep the nonsense from my students though, shield them if you like, so that they can concentrate on the important thing – their karate. I pride myself that the Shotokan I teach today is much the same as the karate I learned under Kanazawa all those years ago. To me that is karate."

VII

THE KANAZAWA LEGACY –
A VERY PERSONAL VIEW

Part II

Michael Randall concluded: "I'm a professional karate instructor, and have been so for thirty years. I'm a lucky man, a very lucky man, because I love my work. I'm not saying that I don't get tired of training and teaching nearly every day, for I sometimes do, especially when I ache, which seems to be most of the time! I believe complaining is human, but I wouldn't swap what I do for the world. What have you got at the end of the day with most jobs? – a pay packet, and that's all. I believe there's more to life than slogging away day after day, year after year, just to put clothes on your back and food in your stomach. There must be more to it than that. Being a karate instructor gives me that extra fulfillment, allows me to self-actualise, to realise my potential. I feel that done properly, karate is a calling that imparts spirit. I'm interested in the correct development, as I see it, of the individual student. I pride myself on that. And I don't mean how well someone can punch or kick. I've taught students who have had wonderful form, but that's all they got from their training, and they left. Karate is not just about technique *per se*; technique is just the tip of the iceberg. Kanazawa *Sensei* taught me that. Technique is the medium through which you train yourself. If karate was as two-dimensional as most people think – you know, self-defence, or worse, competition – I'd have to find something else, but I don't have to because karate has it all.

"If karate is your Way of life, and you train sincerely, any unresolved problems lurking in your mind will naturally come to the surface. If the karateka is pure of heart, whatever is raised can be dealt with through the spirit gained from karate training. Let me give you an example. As I mentioned at the beginning, my initial

Sensei Randall teaching a class at his Winchmore Hill *dojo.*

education was very poor, and I was continually conscious of this. I felt that I had missed out very badly as a child, and I set about trying to improve myself in an intellectual and cultural way. I also found that I needed this to balance what I was practising physically. The karate that I'd learned under Jimmy Neal, Terry Wingrove, and particularly Kanazawa *Sensei* and the other Japanese, had given me confidence and great drive to excel, and I felt that I could improve mentally as well if I was determined enough. I felt that virtually anything was possible.

"My first line of assault to improve my mind was to enrol on an Open University mathematics course. Like a lot of people, I had always found maths a very difficult subject at school, in fact, I couldn't understand it at all beyond 'daily-life maths,' and that's why I decided to enrol on the OU degree course. I wanted to overcome my deficiency, in a similar way that karate had allowed me to overcome my dreadful shyness. I managed a few modules, but I confess that it was wishful thinking believing that I could now undertake such a course. I gave it my best shot, but mathematics was just not my subject, my mind didn't think that way, and I had to admit it. The important thing though was that, having given up the course, I did not, in any way, feel a sense of failure. The problem had been exorcised from me.

"Now, if it's one thing that karate has taught me, it's never to give up. Just because I couldn't fathom the maths, didn't mean that there weren't other subjects out there to interest me. It was at this time that I was invited to join a lodge, and become a Mason. The father of a past student of mine, a 2nd Dan, John Alcock, put my name forward, and I was accepted. This was a major step in my life, like beginning karate, and it was to provide me with the intellectual stimulation that I sought. I now had the means to attain the kind of completeness that I wanted. I was proficient with the sword, if you like, and now I was to be introduced to the pen.

"The Masonic world is really a symbolic one. You are required to learn, by rôte, often lengthy texts that accompany rituals. I have worked very hard at Freemasonry for fifteen years now, and learning these texts and rituals has helped to structure my mind in a way that was not open to me before. The language used in the required texts seems to be from the nineteenth century, and is rich and full of manners of speech that seem quite strange today, with words like parallelepipedon, supererogation, mutule, metope, triglyph, and so on, being referred to. A lot of these odd words are associated with geometry and architecture. I have a love of learning, and in order to understand these texts completely, I did quite a lot of research, and I have many English language and grammar books on my shelves, which I not only consult, but actually actively read. Indirectly, this love of the written word lead me to co-author the three volume, *A Shotokan Karate Book of Facts*, which I confess to being rather proud of. If you had said to me a few years ago that I would be helping writing books, I doubt that I would have believed you. But as Kanazawa *Sensei* used to say to me, "Anything is possible if you really put your mind to it," and that is true."

Michael did not wish to seem self-possessed with importance when the author questioned him further on what he had achieved in the Masons, and was reluctant to discuss the subject for fear that readers would think that he was promoting himself. Eventually, however, the author was able to ascertain that Michael had been a member of ten separate orders of Masonry; was a past master of three different orders – Craft Masonry, Knights Templar and Mark Masonry – and is at present, a master of Royal Ark Mariner Masonry. He is also a Provincial Grand Officer of the Knights Templar, which is a high rank.

Michael continued: "Because in the Masonic world you act out dramas, I found that my *kata* training came in extremely useful. My attention to detail [and a lot of hard work] allowed me to become quite [read "very"] proficient in this field.

It was, partly, Michael Randall's focused attention, derived from his karate training, that allowed his son, Marty, to excel musically. Here, Marty, aged 5, is shown alongside one of his tutors, Fanny Waterman, OBE.

"If you are a full-time karate instructor, it is very easy to live in a kind of bubble, to become isolated; indeed, to spend one's time in an art from a foreign land in a largely forgotten time. You train and mix with the same people, who generally tend to be from a particular walk of life. In Masonry, you meet all sorts of people from very different backgrounds. One minute one could be talking to a cab driver, and the next minute to a High Court Judge. Because of my up-bringing, my education, I would have felt out of my depth in the company of doctors, lawyers, and other professional people. But my karate and my hard work in the Masons has allowed me to mix with any type of person, irrespective of their background and education. Please don't get me wrong here though, the last thing I am concerned with is social climbing, I loathe that type of thing, but mixing with a broader spectrum of people has given me the capacity to take a wider and less emotional view on matters. If you like, studying hard in Freemasonry has given me a new perspective on life which I feel has made me more complete, more wholesome.

"One of the things that both karate and Masonry teach you, is to have a consideration for others. My study of Masonry has definitely affected my karate teaching. I am now more mindful of the students' needs. Sometimes, Freemasonry and karate can overlap in a very practical way. Let me give you an example. Charity work is an important part of being a Mason and I sponsored a child in the Philippines, in that I helped to contribute to his upbringing. I thought it would be nice for the SHOTO association to sponsor a child too, and a small percentage of every licence fee goes to another Philippino child in Calapan. I realise that it is only a tenuous connection, but I think that it's nice for people to know that they are contributing to something worthwhile. When I put it to the students at a christmas dinner, I told them an old Japanese story, which you may have heard: "Once, there was a wise old monk who lived in a remote cave high in the mountains, and in contrast, in the same land, a king, in a fabulous palace, who could not sleep at night for fear that someone would steal his gold. The king, unable to find anyone who could help him resolve his problem, and as a last resort, decided to consult the old monk. The king sent an envoy to the sage, requesting him to come and see the king, but the monk refused. The messenger returned and the king, astonished by the reply, sent another envoy to give the message that the king would come to the mountain to consult the monk instead. The monk once again said that he didn't want to see the king. The king, much perturbed, then decided to go alone to

Michael with SHOTO 6th Dan, John Floyd

consult the monk, and took some gold as a means of payment in respect of the advice he was hoping to receive. After many days of journeying, the monk allowed the weary king to enter the cave, discarding the gold into a dark, damp recess. The king told the monk about his problem – that he was unable to sleep for fear that someone would steal his gold – and the monk replied that he couldn't help him. When the king returned to his palace, he told everyone that the sage was a complete waste of time, and that he hadn't even had the common courtesy to thank him for the gold he had taken. The king repeated his denunciation many times, but then, on one inspired occasion, suddenly saw the light, and laughed aloud, heartily – something he had not done for years. A great weight had been lifted from his shoulders. He had understood that the giver should be thankful, and not the receiver."

"I have some wonderful students. Some of them, especially those who have been training a long time, I regard as members of my family; I really do. They have been brought up in the traditional mould and are very dedicated and very loyal, and the standards they

Michael Randall with the author

maintain are of the highest order. I believe that I could ask them to do anything for me, and that's a wonderful feeling. I suppose that Kanazawa *Sensei* must have felt the same way about his 'samurai' – I hope so. I may not be wealthy financially, but I can assure you that I am a very rich man indeed."

Genuine senior karateka become, in a sense, a breed apart. Through decades of rigorous training, where great physical effort and personal sacrifice are required in the pursuit of an art, a rarely seen human quality emerges, shines, and gently touches all who come into contact with it. Mastery of the virtues of courage, courtesy, integrity, humility and self-control, laid down by Master Funakoshi in his *dojo kun*, knit together to help form a higher-order individual.

Every karateka has the potential to breathe the rarefied air of the Olympian heights. But how many souls, in physical guise, have the dedication to climb, forever upward, the same steep, winding, and often so slippery mountain path, continuously, for a lifetime? Michael Randall is such a man. The author would like to exercise an author's privilege at this late stage, and state that, like a number of other highly selective senior grades, he too is proud to call Michael *"Sensei."*

But perhaps this book should finish with a quote from the man who allowed Michael to take that very first step on the rocky path, in bare feet, all those years ago. Vernon Bell, the founder of British karate, wrote: "Michael has definitely turned out to be exactly as I predicted he would, way back in the early days of karate in this country, at the Horseshoe *dojo*. His loyalty and dedication to the art have led to achievements and experiences that are truly second to none."

Master Hirokazu Kanazawa

ABOUT THE AUTHOR

Clive Layton was born in 1952, and originally started his martial arts training with judo, in 1960, under Terry Wingrove. He began Shotokan karate in 1973 under Mick Randall and the Adamou brothers, Nick and Chris, gaining his black-belt from Hirokazu Kanazawa. Originally attending art school, he later read for both masters' and doctorate degrees from the University of London, and is a Chartered Psychologist and teacher. A prolific writer, with ten much respected karate books and more than sixty articles and research notes to his credit, any spare time he has is taken up flying aeroplanes, salmon fishing in the wilds of Scotland, and enjoying the peace of rural life, by the sea, with his wife, daughter and labrador. A very traditional karateka, he currently holds the rank of 6th Dan.

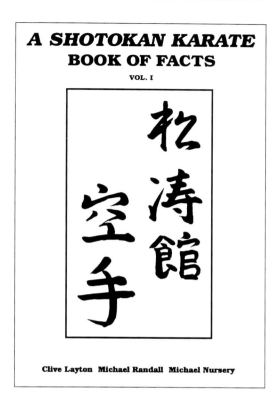

A SHOTOKAN KARATE BOOK OF FACTS is a valuable, easy to access reference work, on general, historical and technical matters. The authors, all respected senior karateka of long standing, have collaborated to produce a much needed and well-researched quality book, which is considered essential reading for students and instructors alike. Who wish to acquire a deeper understanding of their art.

Adopting a question and answer format, Layton, Randall and Nursey have explored a tremendously diverse range of material within their remit. The facts and figures presented, together with the accompanying photographs, allow this unique book to stand proud among the classics in karate publications.

ISBN 0 9530287 0 4

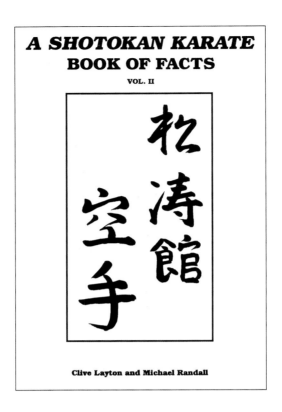

A SHOTOKAN KARATE
BOOK OF FACTS
VOL. II

Clive Layton and Michael Randall

In the wake of the success of Volume 1 of **A SHOTOKAN KARATE
BOOK OF FACTS,** this book continues the tradition of providing a
valuable reference work for students of Shotokan, irrespective of grade, who
wish to acquire a deeper appreciation of their art.

Once again, general, historical and technical information is presented in a
friendly question and answer format, and authors' opinions add much where
interpretation is required. Also included in this volume are signatures of
karateka and budoka important in the development of Shotokan in Great
Britain, before the official coming of the Japan Karate Association. Carefully
worked out kata embusen are additionally provided, which readers are advised
to consult. Historical and detailed photographs accompany the text.

This sequel is one of those rare books that equal the original. A
SHOTOKAN KARATE BOOK OF FACTS is therefore now, rightly, in two
volumes. Layton and Randall have not only made a valuable contribution to
Shotokan by producing this work, they are also to be commended for
making the information accessible to a wide audience.

ISBN 0 9530287 1 2

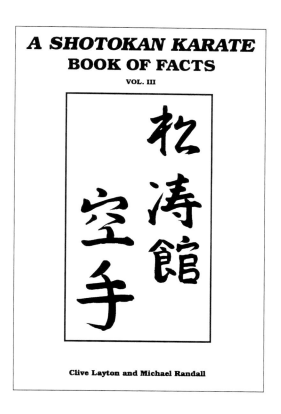

A SHOTOKAN KARATE
BOOK OF FACTS
VOL. III

Clive Layton and Michael Randall

A SHOTOKAN KARATE BOOK OF FACTS: Vol.III brings this exceptional and much appreciated reference work to an end. In all, over five hundred questions - general, historical and technical in nature - have been answered.

Features of the present volume include signatures from selected senior British Shotokan karate-ka holding the rank of sixth dan and above, rare photographs from Japan, the earliest photographs of karate ever published in this country, and Japanese calligraphy. Of course, a whole range of fascinating questions, some quite bizarre, are answered in the same friendly manner that proved so successful in the previous two books. In a few cases, newly acquired information has allowed old gaps in knowledge to be filled, or corrected, and interesting research by the authors, published here for the first time, will open up thoughtful debate. Volume 111 concludes with a valuable three-volume index and terminology section.

Layton, Randall and Nursey (Vol.1 only) have written a series of books that are in a sense, timeless. A SHOTOKAN KARATE BOOK OF FACTS really must be considered essential reading for any thoughtful Shotokan karate-ka. One magazine critic wrote of Vol.I "A 10/10 must buy" and volumes II & III may also be said to fall into this elite category.

ISBN 0 9530287 4 7